SPECIAL MESSAGE TO READERS

This book is published by

THE ULVERSCROFT FOUNDATION

a registered charity in the U.K., No. 264873

The Foundation was established in 1974 to provide funds to help towards research, diagnosis and treatment of eye diseases. Below are a few examples of contributions made by THE ULVERSCROFT FOUNDATION:

A new Children's Assessment Unit at Moorfield's Hospital, London.

•

Twin operating theatres at the Western Ophthalmic Hospital, London.

•

The Frederick Thorpe Ulverscroft Chair of Ophthalmology at the University of Leicester.

•

Eye Laser equipment to various eye hospitals.

If you would like to help further the work of the Foundation by making a donation or leaving a legacy, every contribution, no matter how small, is received with gratitude. Please write for details to:

THE ULVERSCROFT FOUNDATION,
The Green, Bradgate Road, Anstey, Leicester LE7 7FU. England
Telephone: (0533)364325

MACBETH

For his fortitude in defeating Norwegian invaders, King Duncan names Macbeth Thane of Cawdor and condemns the former thane to death as a traitor. Macbeth and Banquo hear of his good fortune from three witches who hail Macbeth as Thane of Glamis, Thane of Cawdor and future king; they tell Banquo he will beget kings but not be one. Ross brings word of Cawdor's fate and Macbeth's elevation. The king promises further rewards, and declares Malcolm, his eldest son, his successor.

The witches' prophecies disturb Macbeth. Knowing the king is to stay at his castle he sends news to Lady Macbeth and rides ahead to prepare. From his letter she realises how he must act but fears he has too much 'milk of human kindness' to kill Duncan. She calls on spirits to unsex her, fill her with cruelty and without remorse. She senses Macbeth is wavering.

The king pays Lady Macbeth a graceful compliment. Macbeth agonizes over his plot to kill Duncan while he is both his king and his guest. Lady Macbeth asks if he fears to do what he knows he must do. She drugs the king's grooms who will bear the guilt of the murder. Macbeth sees a vision of a dagger and prepares for murder. He re-enters with two daggers and hands dripping with blood. Lady Macbeth smears the grooms' faces when Macbeth dare not go back. Someone knocks and they retire to wash their hands. Knocking resumes next day and a drunken porter lets in Macduff and Lennox to rouse the king. Aghast at finding him murdered, they raise the alarm and seek the grooms with Macbeth, who kills them, then admits doing so in his fury. Lady Macbeth faints and in the uproar Malcolm and Donalbain, the king's sons, fly from Scotland. Reports are made of unnatural happenings during the night.

Tortured by the witches' prophecy about Banquo's sons, Macbeth plots to kill Banquo and his son Fleance returning for Macbeth's banquet; Banquo is murdered but Fleance escapes. At the banquet Macbeth is petrified to see Banquo's ghost in his place. He recovers when the ghost disappears, only to return as Macbeth toasts Banquo. The ghost finally vanishes as Macbeth pleads infirmity and the banquet is given over.

Macbeth visits the witches again while they are stirring their cauldron. They tell him to beware Macduff; that no man born of a woman shall harm him; and that he will be king until Birnam Wood comes to Dunsinane. He is shown eight kings, all of

Banquo's line. Learning Macduff has fled he plots to murder Lady Macduff and her sons. Ross warns her Macduff has fled and implores her to follow but she is killed as she flees. Macduff joins Malcolm in England, where Ross brings him the hideous news of his family's murders.

Lady Macbeth walks in her sleep, washing her hands and talking of Duncan and Banquo. Macbeth asks the doctor if he cannot minister to a sick mind; but shortly she dies and Macbeth dwells on the futility of life.

His enemies close in. Malcolm orders every soldier to hold a bough to disguise the size of his army. A terrified servant tells Macbeth that Birnam Wood is moving. Knowing his end is near he kills brave Young Siward in his maiden fight; but his spirit quails when Macduff tells him he was ripped from his mother's womb. He kills Macbeth, and with his head on a pole, hails Malcolm as king. Malcolm names all his thanes earls, and recalls exiled friends to his coronation at Scone.

*Books by William Shakespeare
in the Charnwood Library Series:*

HAMLET
THE MERCHANT OF VENICE
OTHELLO
TWELFTH NIGHT
A MIDSUMMER NIGHT'S DREAM
ROMEO AND JULIET
THE COMEDY OF ERRORS
KING RICHARD THE SECOND
KING HENRY THE FOURTH PART ONE
TITUS ANDRONICUS
JULIUS CAESAR
THE SONNETS
THE TWO GENTLEMEN OF VERONA
AS YOU LIKE IT
KING HENRY THE FOURTH PART TWO
KING HENRY THE FIFTH
TROILUS AND CRESSIDA

WILLIAM SHAKESPEARE

◆

MACBETH

Complete and Unabridged

CHARNWOOD
Leicester

First Charnwood Edition
published May 1994

British Library CIP Data

Shakespeare, William *1564 – 1616*
Macbeth.—Large print ed.—
Charnwood library series
I. Title
822.33

ISBN 0–7089–4509–0

Published by
F. A. Thorpe (Publishing) Ltd.
Anstey, Leicestershire

Set by Words & Graphics Ltd.
Anstey, Leicestershire
Printed and bound in Great Britain by
T. J. Press (Padstow) Ltd., Padstow, Cornwall

This book is printed on acid-free paper

Preface

William Shakespeare

William Shakespeare, born in Stratford-upon-Avon, was the son of John Shakespeare, a native of Snitterfield in Warwickshire, who settled in Henley Street in Stratford, where he traded as glover and merchant. He was elected to the Common Council, rising to hold office as Chamberlain. He became alderman in 1565 and Bailiff in 1568. In 1557 John Shakespeare married Mary Arden, daughter of Robert Arden, a yeoman farmer who had died leaving Mary a house and land at Wilmcote.

John and Mary had eight children, of whom three daughters died in early childhood. William, their third child and eldest son, was born on 23rd April 1564 and baptised in Holy Trinity Church, Stratford, three days later. William's three younger brothers all died comparatively early: only Joan, a younger sister, outlived him.

John Shakespeare's fortunes evidently declined; in 1578 he mortgaged his wife's property at Wilmcote and later was unable to repay the money when it fell due. From 1576 he rarely attended Council meetings and his name was finally removed from the roll of aldermen for non-attendance 'of long time'.

William is likely to have attended Stratford Grammar School, where he would have received a grounding in the 'small Latin and less Greek' Ben Jonson credited him with. While only 18 he married Anne Hathaway, eight years his senior, the daughter of Richard Hathaway, a farmer of nearby Shottery. The marriage took place by licence from the Bishop of Worcester, dated 27th November 1582, probably to avoid delay, as Anne was already pregnant. Their first child, Susanna, born in the following year, was baptised on May 26th; and within two years twins, Hamnet and Judith, were born and were baptised on 2nd February 1585.

How William supported his family in these early years is unknown. With four younger children and a far from thriving business John Shakespeare would look to his eldest son to help in providing for their joint household. Stories told about Shakespeare during these 'lost years' between 1585 and 1592 rely largely on individuals' memories and cannot be verified. One belief is that he was 'a schoolmaster in the country'; another, that he was employed by a country attorney. The legend that he was obliged to leave Stratford after being caught deer-poaching at Charlecote by Sir Thomas Lucy persists, but is similarly unverified.

Whether Shakespeare decided to seek his fortune in London or joined one of the companies of travelling actors that visited Stratford from time to time and so migrated to the London stage, the first mention of him after the birth of his twins is a bitter attack on him by a London playwright, Robert Greene. In a pamphlet written in 1592 Greene warns his fellow playwrights of 'an upstart crow, beautified with our feathers, that with his *tiger's heart wrapped in a player's hide*' (a parody of a line in Shakespeare's *Henry VI Part 3*) 'supposes he is as well able to bombast out a blank verse as the best of you and . . . is in his own conceit the only Shake-scene in a country'. The allusions to Shakespeare are unmistakeable. Friends absolved him of the charge of plagiarism; but the attack reveals that he is already making a mark in the theatre.

In Shakespeare's time neither actors nor theatres were viewed with great favour by those in authority. Actors were obliged to belong to one of the acting companies operating under the protection of a nobleman, to avoid a charge of vagrancy under the Vagrancy Act. Shakespeare belonged to the Lord Chamberlain's Company (later The King's Men) performing before the Queen and Court when called upon. The Company were paid for plays acted at the Lord Chamberlain's behest, their main income coming from takings at performances in the theatres; in Shakespeare's case *The Theatre* in Finsbury; *The Rose* and *The Globe* on Bankside; and later *The Blackfriars Theatre*.

Theatres were considered possible sites of

unrest, vice and disease. Outbreaks of plague closed the theatres frequently. When this occurred in 1593 and 1594, halting the demand for plays, Shakespeare turned his hand to poetry, publishing his two long and successful poems *Venus and Adonis* and *The Rape of Lucrece*, dedicating them both to the influential young Earl of Southampton in terms indicating growing friendship.

In 1594 Shakespeare and Richard Burbage became full members of the Company, a progression that would normally follow an apprenticeship of seven years, though records so early have not survived. Each member held a share in the ownership of the Company, acting members receiving an actor's share of the takings in addition. Plays were written for the Company on contract and the playwright paid by fee, the plays becoming the property of the Company.

Unhappily Shakespeare's growing success in the theatre was marred by family tragedy. In August 1596 his only son Hamnet, one of the twins, died aged only 11; and sadly with him the male line of the Shakespeares died out. His death must have tempered the family's pleasure in the granting of a coat-of-arms to Shakespeare's father, entitling him and his son William to be styled 'Gentleman': a sure sign John Shakespeare's fortunes had recovered, and marking a milestone in our playwright's career. Next year William, then aged 33, bought New

Place, one of the largest houses in Stratford-upon-Avon; tangible proof of his increasing prosperity.

In 1597 theatres were closed by the Privy Council when a comedy *The Isle of Dogs* by Thomas Nashe and Ben Jonson, played at *The Rose* was deemed to be seditious. Jonson and two fellow actors were put in prison.

Shakespeare himself did not escape trouble. His disreputable character Falstaff was originally named Sir John Oldcastle, until Lord Cobham, whose family name was Oldcastle, objected; Shakespeare was obliged to change the name to Falstaff. His play *Richard II* was potentially more dangerous. Shakespeare's scenes leading to Richard II's deposition were thought by some to parallel the political situation of Queen Elizabeth, including the Queen herself. Friends of the Earl of Essex asked the Lord Chamberlain's Men to act *Richard II* in February 1601 on the day before the Earl's abortive uprising against the Queen, for which he was executed. The Privy Council questioned the players closely about the performance but took no action.

John Shakespeare died in 1601 and is buried in Holy Trinity churchyard. In the next few years William strengthened his ties with Stratford. In 1602 he bought a parcel of land in Old Stratford and a cottage in Chapel Lane. In 1605 for the large sum of £450 he was assigned one half of all the tithes of Stratford, Old Stratford, Welcombe and Bishopton, at an annual value of £60.

In 1607 Shakespeare's elder daughter Susanna married John Hall, a rising young physician who built up a substantial practice around Stratford. Their daughter Elizabeth was born next year, shortly before the death of Shakespeare's mother Mary, who is buried with her husband.

In 1608 Richard Burbage and the Company took over *The Blackfriars Theatre* for winter use. *The Globe Theatre* was open to the air and plays were acted by daylight, whereas *The Blackfriars Theatre*, enclosed, provided more comfort for audiences and, with the use of lighting, the opportunity for more elaborate stage effects.

Shakespeare is believed to have returned to live in his native Stratford in 1610 when he was 46, although he continued his association with the theatre for some years longer. It was during a performance of his play *King Henry VIII* in 1613 when cannons were fired at the entrance of the King, that *The Globe Theatre* caught fire and was burnt to the ground, destroying, it is believed, irreplaceable records relating to Shakespeare and The Company.

In 1613 Shakespeare bought a dwelling place near the theatre in Blackfriars, the only property he is known to have bought in London. He seems never to have lived in it and to have rented it to one John Robinson. William Johnson, host of the Mermaid Tavern, John Jackson and John Heminges are named with Shakespeare, but evidently only as trustees. In his will Shakespeare left the property to his daughter Susanna.

In February 1616 Shakespeare's younger daughter, the surviving twin Judith, married Thomas Quiney, the son of his old friend, Richard Quiney; though the revelation of young Quiney's responsibility for the pregnancy of a young woman, Mary Wheeler, clouded the occasion.

Evidently ailing, Shakespeare had given instructions for his will to be drawn up in January. Perhaps doubtful about his new son-in-law's suitability as a husband for Judith, he took steps when revising his will in March to safeguard her position, laying down that one half of her bequest would become payable only when Quiney had settled on his wife lands worth an equivalent amount. This episode and the death of his brother-in-law William Hart, husband of his sister Joan, at the house in Henley Street, may have affected Shakespeare's failing health. Hart was buried on 17th April. Shakespeare died six days later on 23rd April 1616, his 52nd birthday, and was buried on 26th April in the chancel of Holy Trinity Church. His wife survived him by seven years and is buried by his side. His gravestone bears the inscription:

Good friend for Jesus sake forbear
To dig the dust enclosed here:
Blest be the man that spares these stones,
And curst be he that moves my bones.

The popularity of Shakespeare's plays during his lifetime is apparent from the lasting success of the Company, of which he was leading playwright, his own growing prosperity, and the pleasure his plays evidently gave to the Courts of Queen Elizabeth and King James. Printed editions of some of his plays achieved large sales and several reprints.

In his choice of themes he appears to have sensed the moods of the time: the surge of interest in England's past following the defeat of the Armada; a renewed feeling of patriotic fervour and interest in wars at the time of the expedition to Ireland; the perennial enjoyment of comedy and romance; the fashion for plays in Italian settings. After the death of Elizabeth a more sombre outlook emerges; changing in the last group of plays to a mood in which alienation and conflict give way to hope and reconciliation.

The Lord Chamberlain's Company regularly acted before the Queen at Christmas-time. In *A Midsummer Night's Dream* Shakespeare paid a graceful tribute to Her Majesty. There is a tradition that the Queen so enjoyed his portrayal of Falstaff in *Henry IV Parts 1 and 2* that she commanded him to write another play showing Falstaff in love, and requiring it to be ready in a fortnight. Signs of haste in the play, *The Merry Wives of Windsor*, and allusions in the text to an impending great occasion lend colour to this story.

In 1598 Francis Meres, in his *Palladis Tamia*, praised 'mellifluous and honey-tongued Shakespeare' for his *Venus and Adonis*, *Lucrece* and 'sugared Sonnets', ranking his comedies (*Two Gentlemen of Verona*, *Comedy of Errors*, *Love's Labour's Lost*, *Midsummer Night's Dream* and *Merchant of Venice*) with those of Plautus, and his tragedies (*Richard II*, *Richard III*, *Henry IV*, *King John*, *Titus Andronicus* and *Romeo and Juliet*) with those of Seneca.

Upon the accession of King James in 1603 the Lord Chamberlain's Company was authorized to become the King's Men and to play Comedies, Tragedies, Histories, etc., within their usual house *The Globe* and elsewhere. Under King James, who took a keen interest in drama, the King's Men acted more frequently before the Court, performing several plays at Christmas-time. In 1613 *The Tempest* was played before the King for the marriage celebrations of the Princess Elizabeth.

Of the thirty-seven plays believed to be wholly or partly by Shakespeare, nineteen were published in separate quarto editions during his lifetime, *Othello* also being published in this format in 1622. After his death Shakespeare's fellow actors John Heminge, the Company's manager, and Henry Condell undertook the editing of his plays, which were published in one folio volume, The First Folio, in 1623. This volume, including seventeen plays published for the first time contains Shakespeare's complete output of plays, divided into Comedies, Histories and Tragedies; except *Pericles*, which was published in an unauthorized edition in 1609 but omitted from the First Folio.

Ben Jonson, Shakespeare's great rival and candid critic, addressed him in his poem for the First Folio as 'My Beloved, The Author William Shakespeare', writing of him:

'I confess thy writings to be such
As neither man nor muse can praise too much'

and declaring

'He was not of an age but for all time'.

Later critics, including Dryden, Dr. Johnson and Coleridge, in assessing his achievement, have ranked him among the greatest of poets and dramatists.

His appeal today probably owes much to his profound understanding of the human spirit and his ability to represent men's and women's struggles to surmount life's tribulations. His superb delineation of characters must rank among his greatest accomplishments. His foremost roles — Richard III, Macbeth, Hamlet, Falstaff, Othello, Shylock, Lear — are figures of commanding presence, with all their human frailties. Many less prominent figures have unmistakeable identities, delighting or disturbing us in their roles and their relationships with other characters. Shakespeare peopled his plays with heroes and villains; nobles and artisans; learned and simple; young and old; men and women. His soldiers and country-folk bear in their speech the certain stamp of their condition and origins.

Shakespeare's range of themes and dramatic encounters confronts us with moral issues as fresh today as in his own time. Cruelty, treachery, dishonesty and unkindness are starkly portrayed and their protagonists remitted to our judgement. Several plays treat of simple domestic conflicts and trace the uneasy course of true love. His scenes of tenderness reveal a sureness of touch rivalling his mastery of contention and battle. His wit and robust humour are seldom absent from the action even in his tragedies. The plays are written in powerful and rhythmic verse and prose, many including some of the finest passages in our language.

Shakespeare's reputation has grown with the years. His plays have been published in numerous editions, translated into many languages and acted in countries throughout the world. This edition is the first to provide readers with large print copies of his works.

K. J. Rider

From careful study of published texts, performances and associated evidence, the probable
order and approximate dates of composition of
Shakespeare's plays has been established. A table
of his works is appended.

Approximate Dates of Composition of Shakespeare's Works

Plays

By 1592   Henry VI Part 1

By 1594   Henry VI Parts 2 and 3
Richard III
Titus Andronicus
The Comedy of Errors
Love's Labours Lost
The Two Gentlemen of Verona
The Taming of the Shrew

1594–1597 Romeo and Juliet
A Midsummer Night's Dream
Richard II
King John
The Merchant of Venice

1597–1600 Henry IV Parts 1 and 2
Henry V
Much Ado About Nothing
The Merry Wives of Windsor
As You Like It
Julius Caesar
Troilus and Cressida

1601–1603 Hamlet
Twelfth Night
Othello

1603–1608 Measure for Measure
All's Well That Ends Well
King Lear
Macbeth
Timon of Athens
Antony and Cleopatra
Coriolanus

After 1608 Pericles (omitted from the Folio)
Cymbeline
The Winter's Tale
The Tempest

1613 Henry VIII

Poems

MACBETH

Characters.

DUNCAN,	King of Scotland.
MALCOLM,	his sons.
DONALBAIN,	
MACBETH,	generals of
BANQUO,	the King's army.
MACDUFF,	
LENNOX,	
ROSS,	
MENTEITH,	noblemen of Scotland.
ANGUS,	
CAITHNESS,	
FLEANCE,	son to Banquo.
SIWARD,	Earl of Northumberland, general of the English forces.
YOUNG SIWARD,	his son.
SEYTON,	an officer attending on Macbeth.
BOY,	son to Macduff.
AN ENGLISH DOCTOR.	

1

A SCOT DOCTOR.

A SERGEANT.

A PORTER.

AN OLD MAN.

LADY MACBETH.

LADY MACDUFF.

GENTLEWOMAN,   attending on
                  Lady Macbeth.

HECATE.

THREE WITCHES.

APPARITIONS.

LORDS, GENTLEMEN, OFFICERS, SOLDIERS,
MURDERERS, ATTENDANTS, *and* MESSENGERS.

SCENE — in the end of the fourth Act in England;
    through the rest of the play in Scotland.

ACT I

Scene I.

An open place.
Thunder and lightning. Enter three WITCHES.

FIRST WITCH.
　When shall we three meet again
　In thunder, lightning, or in rain?
SECOND WITCH.
　When the hurlyburly's done,
　When the battle's lost and won.
THIRD WITCH.
　That will be ere the set of sun.
FIRST WITCH.
　Where the place?
SECOND WITCH.
　　　　　　　Upon the heath.
THIRD WITCH.
　There to meet with Macbeth.
FIRST WITCH.
　I come, Graymalkin!
SECOND WITCH.
　Paddock calls: — anon!
ALL.
　Fair is foul, and foul is fair:
　Hover through the fog and filthy air.
　　　　　　　　　　　　[*Exeunt.*

5

Scene II.

A camp near Forres.

Alarum within. Enter DUNCAN, MALCOLM, DONALBAIN, LENNOX, *with* ATTENDANTS, *meeting a bleeding* SERGEANT.

DUNCAN.

What bloody man is that? He can report,
As seemeth by his plight, of the revolt
The newest state.

MALCOLM.

This is the sergeant
Who like a good and hardy soldier fought
'Gainst my captivity. — Hail, brave friend!
Say to the king the knowledge of the broil
As thou didst leave it.

SERGEANT.

Doubtful it stood;
As two spent swimmers, that do cling together
And choke their art. The merciless
Macdonwald —
Worthy to be a rebel, for to that
The multiplying villanies of nature
Do swarm upon him — from the western
isles
Of kerns and gallowglasses is supplied;
And fortune, on his damned quarrel smiling,

Show'd like a rebel's whore: but all's too
weak:
For brave Macbeth — well he deserves that
name —
Disdaining fortune, with his brandish'd steel,
Which smoked with bloody execution,
Like valour's minion carved out his passage
Till he faced the slave;
Which ne'er shook hands, nor bade farewell
to him,
Till he unseam'd him from the nave to the
chops,
And fix'd his head upon our battlements.

DUNCAN.
O valiant cousin! worthy gentleman!

SERGEANT.
As whence the sun 'gins his reflection
Shipwrecking storms and direful thunders
break,
So from that spring whence comfort seem'd
to come
Discomfort swells. Mark, king of Scotland,
mark:
No sooner justice had with valour arm'd
Compell'd these skipping kerns to trust their
heels,
But the Norweyan lord, surveying vantage,
With furbish'd arms and new supplies of
men,
Began a fresh assault.

DUNCAN.
                                Dismay'd not this

8

Our captains, Macbeth and Banquo?

SERGEANT.

Yes;

As sparrows eagles, or the hare the lion.
If I say sooth, I must report they were
As cannons overcharged with double cracks,
So they
Doubly redoubled strokes upon the foe:
Except they meant to bathe in reeking
wounds,
Or memorize another Golgotha,
I cannot tell: —
But I am faint, my gashes cry for help.

DUNCAN.

So well thy words become thee as thy wounds;
They smack of honour both. — Go get him
surgeons.

[*Exit* SERGEANT, *attended.*

Who comes here?

Enter ROSS.

MALCOLM.

The worthy thane of Ross.

LENNOX.

What a haste looks through his eyes! So should
he look
That seems to speak things strange.

ROSS.

God save the king!

DUNCAN.

Whence camest thou, worthy thane?

ROSS.

                                    From Fife, great king;
Where the Norweyan banners flout the sky
And fan our people cold. Norway himself,
With terrible numbers,
Assisted by that most disloyal traitor
The thane of Cawdor, began a dismal conflict;
Till that Bellona's bridegroom, lapp'd in proof,
Confronted him with self-comparisons,
Point against point rebellious, arm 'gainst arm,
Curbing his lavish spirit: and, to conclude,
The victory fell on us.

DUNCAN.

                                    Great happiness!

ROSS.

That now
Sweno, the Norways' king, craves composition:
Nor would we deign him burial of his men
Till he disbursed, at Saint Colme's inch,
Ten thousand dollars to our general use.

DUNCAN.

No more that thane of Cawdor shall deceive
Our bosom interest: — go pronounce his
present death,
And with his former title greet Macbeth.

ROSS.

I'll see it done.

DUNCAN.

What he hath lost noble Macbeth hath won.
                                    [*Exeunt.*

Scene III.

A heath near Forres.
Thunder. Enter the three WITCHES.

FIRST WITCH.
Where hast thou been, sister?
SECOND WITCH.
Killing swine.
THIRD WITCH.
Sister, where thou?
FIRST WITCH.
A sailor's wife had chestnuts in her lap,
And munch'd, and munch'd, and munch'd: —
    'Give me,' quoth I:
'Aroint thee, witch!' the rump-fed ronyon
cries.
Her husband's to Aleppo gone, master o' the
Tiger:
But in a sieve I'll thither sail,
And, like a rat without a tail,
I'll do, I'll do, and I'll do.
SECOND WITCH.
I'll give thee a wind.
FIRST WITCH.
Thou'rt kind.
THIRD WITCH.
And I another.

FIRST WITCH.
  I myself have all the other,
  And the very ports they blow,
  All the quarters that they know
  I' the shipman's card.
  I will drain him dry as hay:
  Sleep shall neither night nor day
  Hang upon his pent-house lid;
  He shall live a man forbid:
  Weary se'nnights nine times nine
  Shall he dwindle, peak and pine:
  Though his bark cannot be lost,
  Yet it shall be tempest-tost.
  Look what I have.
SECOND WITCH.
  Show me, show me.
FIRST WITCH.
  Here I have a pilot's thumb,
  Wreck'd as homeward he did come.
                              [*Drum within.*
THIRD WITCH.
  A drum, a drum!
  Macbeth doth come.
ALL.
  The weird sisters, hand in hand,
  Posters of the sea and land,
  Thus do go about, about:
  Thrice to thine and thrice to mine
  And thrice again, to make up nine: —
  Peace! — the charm's wound up.

12

Enter MACBETH *and* BANQUO;
SOLDIERS *at some distance.*

MACBETH.
So foul and fair a day I have not seen.
BANQUO.
How far is't call'd to Forres? — What are
these
So wither'd and so wild in their attire,
That look not like the inhabitants o' the
earth,
And yet are on't? — Live you? or are you
aught
That man may question? You seem to
understand me,
By each at once her chappy finger laying
Upon her skinny lips — you should be
women,
And yet your beards forbid me to interpret
That you are so.
MACBETH.
                 Speak, if you can; — what are you?
FIRST WITCH.
All hail, Macbeth! hail to thee, thane of
Glamis!
SECOND WITCH.
All hail, Macbeth, hail to thee, thane of
Cawdor!
THIRD WITCH.
All hail, Macbeth, that shalt be king hereafter!
BANQUO.
Good sir, why do you start; and seem to fear

Things that do sound so fair? — I' the name
of truth,
Are ye fantastical, or that indeed
Which outwardly ye show? My noble partner
You greet with present grace and great
prediction
Of noble having and of royal hope,
That he seems rapt withal: — to me you
speak not.
If you can look into the seeds of time,
And say which grain will grow and which
will not,
Speak then to me, who neither beg nor
fear
Your favours nor your hate.

FIRST WITCH.
Hail!

SECOND WITCH.
Hail!

THIRD WITCH.
Hail!

FIRST WITCH.
Lesser than Macbeth, and greater.

SECOND WITCH.
Not so happy, yet much happier.

THIRD WITCH.
Thou shalt get kings, though thou be none:
So all hail, Macbeth and Banquo!

FIRST WITCH.
Banquo and Macbeth, all hail!

MACBETH.
Stay, you imperfect speakers, tell me more:

By Sinel's death I know I am thane of
Glamis;
But how of Cawdor? the thane of Cawdor
lives,
A prosperous gentleman; and to be king
Stands not within the prospect of belief,
No more than to be Cawdor. Say from
whence
You owe this strange intelligence? or why
Upon this blasted heath you stop our way
With such prophetic greeting? Speak, I charge
you.

[*Witches vanish.*

BANQUO.

The earth hath bubbles, as the water has,
And these are of them. — whither are they
vanish'd?

MACBETH.

Into the air; and what seem'd corporal melted
As breath into the wind. — Would they had
stay'd!

BANQUO.

Were such things here as we do speak about?
Or have we eaten on the insane root
That takes the reason prisoner?

MACBETH.

Your children shall be kings.

BANQUO.

You shall be king.

MACBETH.

And thane of Cawdor too, — went it not
so?

BANQUO.

   To the selfsame tune and words. — Who's
here?

        Enter ROSS *and* ANGUS.

ROSS.

   The king hath happily received, Macbeth,
   The news of thy success; and when he reads
   Thy personal venture in the rebels' fight,
   His wonders and his praises do contend
   Which should be thine or his: silenced with
   that,
   In viewing o'er the rest o' the selfsame day,
   He finds thee in the stout Norweyan ranks,
   Nothing afeard of what thyself didst make,
   Strange images of death. As thick as hail
   Came post with post; and every one did
   bear
   Thy praises in his kingdom's great defence,
   And pour'd them down before him.

ANGUS.

                       We are sent
   To give thee from our royal master, thanks;
   Only to herald thee into his sight,
   Not pay thee.

ROSS.

   And, for an earnest of a greater honour,
   He bade me, from him, call thee thane of
   Cawdor:
   In which addition, hail, most worthy thane!
   For it is thine.

BANQUO.
What, can the devil speak true?
MACBETH.
The thane of Cawdor lives: why do you dress me
In borrow'd robes?
ANGUS.
                                Who was the thane lives yet;
But under heavy judgment bears that life
Which he deserves to lose. Whether he was combined
With those of Norway, or did line the rebel
With hidden help and vantage, or that with both
He labour'd in his country's wreck, I know not;
But treasons capital, confess'd and proved,
Have overthrown him.
MACBETH [aside].
                                Glamis, and thane of Cawdor!
The greatest is behind. — [to ROSS and ANGUS]
        Thanks for your pains. —
[aside to BANQUO] Do you not hope your children shall be kings,
When those that gave the thane of Cawdor to me
Promised no less to them?
BANQUO [aside to MACBETH].
                                That, trusted home,
Might yet enkindle you unto the crown,
Besides the thane of Cawdor. But 'tis strange:

17

And oftentimes, to win us to our harm,
The instruments of darkness tell us truths,
Win us with honest trifles, to betray's
In deepest consequence. —
Cousins, a word, I pray you.
MACBETH [*aside*].

                             Two truths are told,
As happy prologues to the swelling act
Of the imperial theme. — I thank you,
gentlemen. —
[*aside*] This supernatural soliciting
Cannot be ill, cannot be good: — if ill,
Why hath it given me earnest of success,
Commencing in a truth? I am thane of
Cawdor:
If good, why do I yield to that suggestion
Whose horrid image doth unfix my hair
And make my seated heart knock at my
ribs,
Against the use of nature? Present fears
Are less than horrible imaginings:
My thought, whose murder yet is but
fantastical,
Shakes so my single state of man that function
Is smother'd in surmise, and nothing is
But what is not.
BANQUO.

                        Look, how our partner's rapt.
MACBETH [*aside*].
If chance will have me king, why, chance may
crown me,
Without my stir.

BANQUO.
>   New honours come upon him,
Like our strange garments, cleave not to their mould
But with the aid of use.

MACBETH [*aside*].
>   Come what come may,
Time and the hour runs through the roughest day.

BANQUO.
Worthy Macbeth, we stay upon your leisure.

MACBETH.
Give me your favour: — my dull brain was wrought
With things forgotten. Kind gentlemen, your pains
Are register'd where every day I turn
The leaf to read them. — Let us toward the king. —
[*aside to* BANQUO] Think upon what hath chanced, and, at more time,
The interim having weigh'd it, let us speak
Our free hearts each to other.

BANQUO [*aside to* MACBETH].
>   Very gladly.

MACBETH.
Till then, enough. — Come, friends.
>   [*Exeunt.*

Scene IV.

Forres. A room in the palace.
Flourish. Enter DUNCAN, MALCOLM, DONALBAIN,
LENNOX, *and* ATTENDANTS.

DUNCAN.
Is execution done on Cawdor? Are not
Those in commission yet return'd?
MALCOLM.

                          My liege,
They are not yet come back. But I have
spoke
With one that saw him die: who did report
That very frankly he confess'd his treasons,
Implored your highness' pardon and set forth
A deep repentance: nothing in his life
Became him like the leaving it; he died
As one that had been studied in his death
To throw away the dearest thing he owed,
As 'twere a careless trifle.
DUNCAN.

                        There's no art
To find the mind's construction in the face:
He was a gentleman on whom I built
An absolute trust.

Enter MACBETH, BANQUO, ROSS, *and* ANGUS.

21

O worthiest cousin!
The sin of my ingratitude even now
Was heavy on me: thou art so far before,
That swiftest wing of recompense is slow
To overtake thee. Would thou hadst less deserved,
That the proportion both of thanks and payment
Might have been mine! only I have left to say,
More is thy due than more than all can pay.
MACBETH.
The service and the loyalty I owe,
In doing it, pays itself. Your highness' part
Is to receive our duties; and our duties
Are to your throne and state children and servants,
Which do but what they should, by doing every thing
Safe toward your love and honour.
DUNCAN.
                                   Welcome hither:
I have begun to plant thee, and will labour
To make thee full of growing. — Noble Banquo,
That hast no less deserved, nor must be known
No less to have done so; let me enfold thee
And hold thee to my heart.
BANQUO.
                                   There if I grow,
The harvest is your own.

DUNCAN.

                              My plenteous joys,
Wanton in fulness, seek to hide themselves
In drops of sorrow. — Sons, kinsmen, thanes,
And you whose places are the nearest, know
We will establish our estate upon
Our eldest, Malcolm, whom we name hereafter
The Prince of Cumberland; which honour
must
Not unaccompanied invest him only,
But signs of nobleness, like stars, shall shine
On all deservers. — From hence to Inverness,
And bind us further to you.

MACBETH.

The rest is labour, which is not used for
you:
I'll be myself the harbinger and make joyful
The hearing of my wife with your approach;
So humbly take my leave.

DUNCAN.

                              My worthy Cawdor!

MACBETH [*aside*].

The Prince of Cumberland! that is a step
On which I must fall down, or else o'erleap,
For in my way it lies. Stars, hide your fires;
Let not light see my black and deep desires:
The eye wink at the hand; yet let that be,
Which the eye fears, when it is done, to
see.

                                        [*Exit.*

DUNCAN.

True, worthy Banquo; — he is full so valiant,

And in his commendations I am fed; —
It is a banquet to me. Let's after him,
Whose care is gone before to bid us welcome:
It is a peerless kinsman.

[*Flourish. Exeunt.*

Scene V.

Inverness. A room in MACBETH'S castle.
Enter LADY MACBETH, *reading a letter.*

LADY MACBETH.
'They met me in the day of success: and I
have learned by the perfectest report, they
have more in them than mortal knowledge.
When I burned in desire to question them
further, they made themselves air, into which
they vanished. Whiles I stood rapt in the
wonder of it, came missives from the king,
who all-hailed me "Thane of Cawdor;" by
which title, before, these weird sisters saluted
me, and referred me to the coming on of time,
with "Hail, king that shalt be!" This have
I thought good to deliver thee, my dearest
partner of greatness, that thou mightst not
lose the dues of rejoicing, by being ignorant
of what greatness is promised thee. Lay it to
thy heart, and farewell.'
Glamis thou art, and Cawdor; and shalt be
What thou art promised: yet do I fear thy
nature;
It is too full o' the milk of human kindness
To catch the nearest way: thou wouldst be
great;

Art not without ambition, but without
The illness should attend it: what thou wouldst
highly,
That wouldst thou holily; wouldst not play
false,
And yet wouldst wrongly win: thou'ldst have,
great Glamis,
That which cries 'Thus thou must do, if thou
have it;
And that which rather thou dost fear to do
Than wishest should be undone.' Hie thee
hither,
That I may pour my spirits in thine ear;
And chastise with the valour of my tongue
All that impedes thee from the golden round,
Which fate and metaphysical aid doth seem
To have thee crown'd withal.

Enter a MESSENGER.

           What is your tidings?

MESENGER.
The king comes here tonight.

LADY MACBETH.
           Thou'rt mad to say it:
Is not thy master with him? who, were't
so,
Would have inform'd for preparation.

MESENGER.
So please you, it is true: — our thane is
coming:
One of my fellows had the speed of him;

Who, almost dead for breath, had scarcely more
Than would make up his message.

LADY MACBETH.

                          Give him tending;
He brings great news.

                         [*Exit* MESSENGER.

The raven himself is hoarse
That croaks the fatal entrance of Duncan
Under my battlements. Come, you spirits
That tend on mortal thoughts, unsex me here,
And fill me, from the crown to the toe, top-full
Of direst cruelty! make thick my blood;
Stop up the access and passage to remorse,
That no compunctious visitings of nature
Shake my fell purpose, nor keep peace between
The effect and it! Come to my woman's breasts,
And take my milk for gall, you murdering ministers,
Wherever in your sightless substances
You wait on nature's mischief! Come, thick night,
And pall thee in the dunnest smoke of hell,
That my keen knife see not the wound it makes,
Nor heaven peep through the blanket of the dark,
To cry 'Hold, hold!'

Enter MACBETH.

            Great Glamis! worthy Cawdor!
Greater than both, by the all-hail hereafter!
Thy letters have transported me beyond
This ignorant present, and I feel now
The future in the instant.
MACBETH.
                       My dearest love,
Duncan comes here tonight.
LADY MACBETH.
                   And when goes hence?
MACBETH.
Tomorrow, as he purposes.
LADY MACBETH.
                       O, never
Shall sun that morrow see!
Your face, my thane, is as a book where men
May read strange matters: — to beguile the time,
Look like the time; bear welcome in your eye,
Your hand, your tongue: look like the innocent flower,
But be the serpent under't. He that's coming
Must be provided for: and you shall put
This night's great business into my dispatch;
Which shall to all our nights and days to come
Give solely sovereign sway and masterdom.
MACBETH.
We will speak further.

LADY MACBETH.

                     Only look up clear;
To alter favour ever is to fear:
Leave all the rest to me.
                         [*Exeunt.*

Scene VI.

The same. Before MACBETH'S castle.
Hautboys and torches. Enter DUNCAN,
MALCOLM, DONALBAIN, BANQUO, LENNOX,
MACDUFF, ROSS, ANGUS, *and* ATTENDANTS.

DUNCAN.
This castle hath a pleasant seat; the air
Nimbly and sweetly recommends itself
Unto our gentle senses.
BANQUO.
                              This guest of summer,
The temple-haunting martlet, does approve,
By his loved mansionry, that the heaven's
breath
Smells wooingly here: no jutty, frieze,
Buttress, nor coign of vantage, but this bird
Hath made his pendent bed and procreant
cradle:
Where they most breed and haunt, I have
observed,
The air is delicate.

Enter LADY MACBETH.

DUNCAN.
                              See, see, our honour'd hostess! —

31

The love that follows us sometime is our trouble,
Which still we thank as love. Herein I teach you
How you shall bid God 'ild us for your pains,
And thank us for your trouble.

LADY MACBETH.
                                    All our service
In every point twice done, and then done double,
Were poor and single business to contend
Against those honours deep and broad wherewith
Your majesty loads our house: for those of old,
And the late dignities heap'd up to them,
We rest your hermits.

DUNCAN.
                        Where's the thane of Cawdor?
We coursed him at the heels, and had a purpose
To be his purveyor: but he rides well;
And his great love, sharp as his spur, hath holp him
To his home before us. Fair and noble hostess,
We are your guest tonight.

LADY MACBETH.
                            Your servants ever
Have theirs, themselves and what is theirs, in count,

To make their audit at your highness'
pleasure,
Still to return your own.

DUNCAN.

Give me your hand;
Conduct me to mine host: we love him
highly,
And shall continue our graces towards him.
By your leave, hostess.

[*Exeunt.*

Scene VII.

The same. A lobby in MACBETH'S castle.
Hautboys and torches. Enter a SEWER, *and
divers.* SERVANTS *with dishes and service pass
over the stage. Then enter* MACBETH.

MACBETH.

If it were done — when 'tis done — then
'twere well
It were done quickly: if the assassination
Could trammel up the consequence, and
catch
With his surcease success; that but this blow
Might be the be-all and the end-all here,
But here, upon this bank and shoal of time,
We'ld jump the life to come. But in these
cases
We still have judgment here; that we but
teach
Bloody instructions, which, being taught,
return
To plague the inventor: this even-handed
justice
Commends the ingredients of our poison'd
chalice
To our own lips. He's here in double trust;
First, as I am his kinsman and his subject,

Strong both against the deed; then, as his host,
Who should against his murderer shut the door,
Not bear the knife myself. Besides, this Duncan
Hath borne his faculties so meek, hath been
So clear in his great office, that his virtues
Will plead like angels, trumpet-tongued, against
The deep damnation of his taking-off;
And pity, like a naked new-born babe,
Striding the blast, or heaven's cherubim, horsed
Upon the sightless couriers of the air,
Shall blow the horrid deed in every eye,
That tears shall drown the wind. I have no spur
To prick the sides of my intent, but only
Vaulting ambition, which o'erleaps itself
And falls on the other.

Enter LADY MACBETH.

How now! what news?

LADY MACBETH.
He has almost supp'd: why have you left the chamber?

MACBETH.
Hath he ask'd for me?

LADY MACBETH.
Know you not he has?

36

MACBETH.
We will proceed no further in this business:
He hath honour'd me of late; and I have bought
Golden opinions from all sorts of people,
Which would be worn now in their newest gloss,
Not cast aside so soon.

LADY MACBETH.
                              Was the hope drunk
Wherein you dress'd yourself? hath it slept since?
And wakes it now, to look so green and pale
At what it did so freely? From this time
Such I account thy love. Art thou afeard
To be the same in thine own act and valour
As thou art in desire? Wouldst thou have that
Which thou esteem'st the ornament of life,
And live a coward in thine own esteem,
Letting 'I dare not' wait upon 'I would,'
Like the poor cat i' the adage?

MACBETH.
                              Prithee, peace:
I dare do all that may become a man;
Who dares do more is none.

LADY MACBETH.
                              What beast was't, then,
That made you break this enterprise to me?
When you durst do it, then you were a man;

37

And, to be more than what you were, you
would
Be so much more the man. Nor time nor
place
Did then adhere, and yet you would make
both:
They have made themselves, and that their
fitness now
Does unmake you. I have given suck, and
know
How tender 'tis to love the babe that milks
me:
I would, while it was smiling in my face,
Have pluck'd my nipple from his boneless
gums,
And dash'd the brains out, had I so sworn
as you
Have done to this.

MACBETH.
                          If we should fail?

LADY MACBETH.
                                    We fail:
But screw your courage to the sticking-place,
And we'll not fail. When Duncan is asleep —
Whereto the rather shall his day's hard journey
Soundly invite him — his two chamberlains
Will I with wine and wassail so convince
That memory, the warder of the brain,
Shall be a fume, and the receipt of reason
A limbeck only: when in swinish sleep
Their drenched natures lie as in a death,
What cannot you and I perform upon

The unguarded Duncan? what not put upon
His spongy officers, who shall bear the guilt
Of our great quell?

MACBETH.

               Bring forth men-children only;
For thy undaunted mettle should compose
Nothing but males. Will it not be received,
When we have mark'd with blood those
sleepy two
Of his own chamber and used their very
daggers,
That they have done't?

LADY MACBETH.

               Who dares receive it other,
As we shall make our griefs and clamour
roar
Upon his death?

MACBETH.

               I am settled, and bend up
Each corporal agent to this terrible feat.
Away, and mock the time with fairest show:
False face must hide what the false heart doth
know.

                        [*Exeunt.*

ACT II

Scene I.

Inverness. Court of MACBETH'S *castle.*
Enter BANQUO, *and* FLEANCE *bearing*
a torch before him.

BANQUO.
How goes the night, boy?
FLEANCE.
The moon is down; I have not heard the
clock.
BANQUO.
And she goes down at twelve.
FLEANCE.
           I take't, 'tis later, sir.
BANQUO.
Hold, take my sword. — there's husbandry in
heaven;
Their candles are all out: — take thee that
too. —
A heavy summons lies like lead upon me,
And yet I would not sleep: — merciful
powers,
Restrain in me the cursed thoughts that
nature
Gives way to in repose! — Give me my
sword, —
Who's there?

Enter MACBETH, *and a* SERVANT *with a torch.*

MACBETH.
   A friend.
BANQUO.
   What, sir, not yet at rest? The king's a-bed:
   He hath been in unusual pleasure, and
   Sent forth great largess to your offices.
   This diamond he greets your wife withal,
   By the name of most kind hostess; and shut
   up
   In measureless content.
MACBETH.
                                    Being unprepared,
   Our will became the servant to defect;
   Which else should free have wrought.
BANQUO.
                                    All's well. —
   I dreamt last night of the three weird sisters:
   To you they have show'd some truth.
MACBETH.
                          I think not of them:
   Yet, when we can entreat an hour to serve,
   We would spend it in some words upon that
   business,
   If you would grant the time.
BANQUO.
                          At your kind'st leisure.
MACBETH.
   If you shall cleave to my consent, — when
   'tis,
   It shall make honour for you.

BANQUO.

                                        So I lose none
In seeking to augment it, but still keep
My bosom franchised and allegiance clear,
I shall be counsell'd.

MACBETH.

                        Good repose the while!

BANQUO.

Thanks, sir: the like to you!

                [Exeunt BANQUO *and* FLEANCE.

MACBETH.

Go bid thy mistress, when my drink is ready,
She strike upon the bell. Get thee to bed.

                        [Exit SERVANT.

Is this a dagger which I see before me,
The handle toward my hand? Come, let me clutch thee: —
I have thee not, and yet I see thee still.
Art thou not, fatal vision, sensible
To feeling as to sight? or art thou but
A dagger of the mind, a false creation,
Proceeding from the heat-oppressed brain?
I see thee yet, in form as palpable
As this which now I draw.
Thou marshall'st me the way that I was going;
And such an instrument I was to use.
Mine eyes are made the fools o' the other senses,
Or else worth all the rest; I see thee still,
And on thy blade and dudgeon gouts of blood,

Which was not so before. — There's no such
thing:
It is the bloody business which informs
Thus to mine eyes. — Now o'er the one
half-world
Nature seems dead, and wicked dreams abuse
The curtain'd sleep; witchcraft celebrates
Pale Hecate's offerings; and wither'd murder,
Alarum'd by his sentinel, the wolf,
Whose howl's his watch, thus with his stealthy
pace,
With Tarquin's ravishing strides, towards his
design
Moves like a ghost. — Thou sure and firm-set
earth,
Hear not my steps, which way they walk,
for fear
Thy very stones prate of my whereabout,
And take the present horror from the time,
Which now suits with it. — Whiles I threat,
he lives:
Words to the heat of deeds too cold breath
gives.

                                      [*A bell rings.*

I go, and it is done; the bell invites me.
Hear it not, Duncan; for it is a knell
That summons thee to heaven or to hell.

                                            [*Exit.*

Scene II.

The same.
Enter LADY MACBETH.

LADY MACBETH.

That which hath made them drunk hath made
me bold;
What hath quench'd them hath given me
fire. —
Hark! Peace!
It was the owl that shriek'd, the fatal bellman,
Which gives the stern'st good-night. — He is
about it:
The doors are open; and the surfeited grooms
Do mock their charge with snores: I have
drugg'd their possets,
That death and nature do contend about
them,
Whether they live or die.

MACBETH [*within*].

Who's there? what, ho!

LADY MACBETH.

Alack, I am afraid they have awaked,
And 'tis not done: — The attempt and not
the deed
Confounds us. — Hark! — I laid their daggers
ready;

47

He could not miss 'em. — Had he not
resembled
My father as he slept, I had done't. — My
husband!

Enter MACBETH.

MACBETH.
I have done the deed. — Didst thou not hear
a noise?
LADY MACBETH.
I heard the owl scream and the crickets
cry.
Did not you speak?
MACBETH.
                            When?
LADY MACBETH.
                             Now.
MACBETH.
                  As I descended?
LADY MACBETH.
Ay.
MACBETH.
Hark! —
Who lies i' the second chamber?
LADY MACBETH.
                  Donalbain.
MACBETH.
This is a sorry sight.
                [Looking on his hands.
LADY MACBETH.
A foolish thought, to say a sorry sight.

48

MACBETH.

There's one did laugh in's sleep, and one cried
'Murder!'
That they did wake each other: I stood and
heard them:
But they did say their prayers, and address'd
them
Again to sleep.

LADY MACBETH.

               There are two lodged together.

MACBETH.

One cried 'God bless us!' and 'Amen' the
other;
As they had seen me with these hangman's
hands.
Listening their fear, I could not say 'Amen,'
When they did say 'God bless us!'

LADY MACBETH.

               Consider it not so deeply.

MACBETH.

But wherefore could not I pronounce 'Amen'?
I had most need of blessing, and 'Amen'
Stuck in my throat.

LADY MACBETH.

               These deeds must not be thought
After these ways; so, it will make us mad.

MACBETH.

Methought I heard a voice cry 'Sleep no
more!
Macbeth does murder sleep', — the innocent
sleep,
Sleep that knits up the ravell'd sleeve of care,

The death of each day's life, sore labour's
bath,
Balm of hurt minds, great nature's second
course,
Chief nourisher in life's feast, —

LADY MACBETH.

What do you mean?

MACBETH.

Still it cried 'Sleep no more!' to all the
house:
'Glamis hath murder'd sleep, and therefore
Cawdor
Shall sleep no more; Macbeth shall sleep no
more.'

LADY MACBETH.

Who was it that thus cried? Why, worthy
thane,
You do unbend your noble strength, to think
So brainsickly of things. — Go get some
water,
And wash this filthy witness from your
hand. —
Why did you bring these daggers from the
place?
They must lie there: go carry them; and smear
The sleepy grooms with blood.

MACBETH.

I'll go no more:
I am afraid to think what I have done;
Look on't again I dare not.

LADY MACBETH.

Infirm of purpose!

Give me the daggers: the sleeping and the
dead
Are but as pictures: 'tis the eye of childhood
That fears a painted devil. If he do bleed,
I'll gild the faces of the grooms withal;
For it must seem their guilt.

                        [*Exit. Knock within.*

MACBETH.

                    Whence is that knocking?
How is't with me, when every noise appals
me?
What hands are here? ha! they pluck out
mine eyes.
Will all great Neptune's ocean wash this
blood
Clean from my hand? No, this my hand will
rather
The multitudinous seas incarnadine,
Making the green one red.

                Enter LADY MACBETH.

LADY MACBETH.
My hands are of your colour; but I shame
To wear a heart so white. [*Knock.*] I hear a
knocking
At the south entry: retire we to our chamber;
A little water clears us of this deed:
How easy is it, then! Your constancy
Hath left you unattended.—[*Knock.*] Hark!
more knocking:
Get on your nightgown, lest occasion call us,

And show us to be watchers: — be not lost
So poorly in your thoughts.

MACBETH.

To know my deed, 'twere best not know
myself.

[*Knock.*

Wake Duncan with thy knocking! I would
thou couldst!

[*Exeunt.*

Scene III.

The same.
Enter a PORTER. *Knocking within.*

PORTER.

Here's a knocking indeed! If a man were porter of hell-gate, he should have old turning the key. — [*Knock.*] Knock, knock, knock! Who's there, i' the name of Beelzebub? Here's a farmer, that hanged himself on the expectation of plenty: come in time; have napkins enow about you; here you'll sweat for't. [*Knock.*] Knock, knock! Who's there, in th'other devil's name? Faith, here's an equivocator, that could swear in both the scales against either scale; who committed treason enough for God's sake, yet could not equivocate to heaven: O, come in, equivocator. — [*Knock.*] Knock, knock, knock! Who's there? Faith, here's an English tailor come hither, for stealing out of a French hose: come in, tailor; here you may roast your goose. — [*Knock.*] Knock, knock; never at quiet! What are you? But this place is too cold for hell. I'll devil-porter it no further: I had thought to have let in some of all professions that go the primrose way to the everlasting bonfire. — [*Knock.*] Anon,

53

anon! I pray you, remember the porter.

[*Opens the gate.*

Enter MACDUFF *and* LENNOX.

MACDUFF.
Was it so late, friend, ere you went to bed,
That you do lie so late?
PORTER.
'Faith sir, we were carousing till the second
cock: and drink, sir, is a great provoker of
three things.
MACDUFF.
What three things does drink especially
provoke?
PORTER.
Marry, sir, nose-painting, sleep, and urine.
Lechery, sir, it provokes, and unprovokes; it
provokes the desire, but it takes away the
performance: therefore, much drink may be
said to be an equivocator with lechery: it
makes him, and it mars him; it sets him on,
and it takes him off; it persuades him, and
disheartens him; makes him stand to, and not
stand to; in conclusion, equivocates him in a
sleep, and, giving him the lie, leaves him.
MACDUFF.
I believe drink gave thee the lie last night.
PORTER.
That it did, sir, i' the very throat on me: but
I requited him for his lie; and, I think, being
too strong for him, though he took up my legs

sometime, yet I made a shift to cast him.

MACDUFF.
Is thy master stirring? —

Enter MACBETH.

Our knocking has awaked him; here he comes.

LENNOX.
Good morrow, noble sir.

MACBETH.
                              Good morrow, both.

MACDUFF.
Is the king stirring, worthy thane?

MACBETH.
                                        Not yet.

MACDUFF.
He did command me to call timely on him:
I have almost slipp'd the hour.

MACBETH.
                              I'll bring you to him.

MACDUFF.
I know this is a joyful trouble to you;
But yet 'tis one.

MACBETH.
The labour we delight in physics pain.
This is the door.

MACDUFF.
                  I'll make so bold to call,
For 'tis my limited service.

                                        [*Exit.*

LENNOX.

Goes the king hence today?

MACBETH.

He does: he did appoint so.

LENNOX.

The night has been unruly: where we lay,
Our chimneys were blown down; and, as
they say,
Lamentings heard i' the air; strange screams
of death,
And prophesying with accents terrible
Of dire combustion and confused events
New hatch'd to the woeful time: the obscure
bird
Clamour'd the livelong night: some say, the
earth
Was feverous and did shake.

MACBETH.

'Twas a rough night.

LENNOX.

My young remembrance cannot parallel
A fellow to it.

Enter MACDUFF.

MACDUFF.

O horror, horror, horror! Tongue nor heart
Cannot conceive nor name thee!

MACBETH *and* LENNOX.

What's the matter.

MACDUFF.

Confusion now hath made his masterpiece!

Most sacrilegious murder hath broke ope
The Lord's anointed temple, and stole thence
The life o' the building!

MACBETH.

      What is 't you say? the life?

LENNOX.

Mean you his majesty?

MACDUFF.

Approach the chamber, and destroy your
sight
With a new Gorgon: — do not bid me speak;
See, and then speak yourselves.

      [Exeunt MACBETH *and* LENNOX.

      Awake, awake!
Ring the alarum-bell: — murder and treason! —
Banquo and Donalbain! Malcolm! awake!
Shake off this downy sleep, death's counterfeit,
And look on death itself! up, up, and see
The great doom's image! Malcolm! Banquo!
As from your graves rise up, and walk like
sprites,
To countenance this horror!

       [Bell rings.

Enter LADY MACBETH.

LADY MACBETH.

What's the business,
That such a hideous trumpet calls to parley
The sleepers of the house? speak, speak!

MACDUFF.

O gentle lady,

57

'Tis not for you to hear what I can speak:
The repetition, in a woman's ear,
Would murder as it fell.

Enter BANQUO.

                    O Banquo, Banquo,
Our royal master 's murder'd!
LADY MACBETH.

                                        Woe, alas!
What, in our house?
BANQUO.

                              Too cruel any where. —
Dear Duff, I prithee, contradict thyself,
And say it is not so.

Enter MACBETH *and* LENNOX, *with* ROSS.

MACBETH.
Had I but died an hour before this chance,
I had lived a blessed time; for, from this
instant,
There 's nothing serious in mortality:
All is but toys: renown and grace is dead;
The wine of life is drawn, and the mere
lees
Is left this vault to brag of.

Enter MALCOLM *and* DONALBAIN.

DONALBAIN.
What is amiss?

MACBETH.

              You are, and do not know't:
The spring, the head, the fountain of your blood
Is stopp'd, — the very source of it is stopp'd.

MACDUFF.

Your royal father's murder'd.

MALCOLM.

                      O, by whom?

LENNOX.

Those of his chamber, as it seem'd, had done 't:
Their hands and faces were all badged with blood;
So were their daggers, which unwiped we found
Upon their pillows:
They stared, and were distracted; no man's life
Was to be trusted with them.

MACBETH.

O, yet I do repent me of my fury,
That I did kill them.

MACDUFF.

                  Wherefore did you so?

MACBETH.

Who can be wise, amazed, temperate and furious,
Loyal and neutral, in a moment? No man:
The expedition my violent love
Outrun the pauser, reason. Here lay Duncan,
His silver skin laced with his golden blood;

And his gash'd stabs look'd like a breach in
nature
For ruin's wasteful entrance: there, the
murderers,
Steep'd in the colours of their trade, their
daggers
Unmannerly breech'd with gore: who could
refrain,
That had a heart to love, and in that heart
Courage to make's love known?

LADY MACBETH.

Help me hence, ho!

MACDUFF.

Look to the lady.

MALCOLM [*aside to* DONALBAIN].

Why do we hold our tongues,
That most may claim this argument for
ours?

DONALBAIN [*aside to* MALCOLM].

What should be spoken here, where our fate,
Hid in an auger-hole, may rush, and seize
us?
Let's away;
Our tears are not yet brew'd.

MALCOLM [*aside to* DONALBAIN].

Nor our strong sorrow
Upon the foot of motion.

BANQUO.

Look to the lady: —

[LADY MACBETH *is carried out.*

And when we have our naked frailties hid,
That suffer in exposure, let us meet,

And question this most bloody piece of work,
To know it further. Fears and scruples shake us:
In the great hand of God I stand; and thence
Against the undivulged pretence I fight
Of treasonous malice.

MACDUFF.

                And so do I.

ALL.

                      So all.

MACBETH.
Let's briefly put on manly readiness,
And meet i' the hall together.

ALL.

                Well contented.

    [*Exeunt all but* MALCOLM *and* DONALBAIN.

MALCOLM.
What will you do? Let's not consort with them:
To show an unfelt sorrow is an office
Which the false man does easy. I'll to England.

DONALBAIN.
To Ireland, I; our separated fortune
Shall keep us both the safer: where we are,
There's daggers in men's smiles: the near in blood,
The nearer bloody.

MALCOLM.

         This murderous shaft that's shot

Hath not yet lighted, and our safest way
Is to avoid the aim. Therefore, to horse;
And let us not be dainty of leave-taking,
But shift away: there's warrant in that theft
Which steals itself, when there's no mercy
left.

[*Exeunt.*

Scene IV.

Outside MACBETH'S castle.
Enter ROSS *and an* OLD MAN.

OLD MAN.

Threescore and ten I can remember well:
Within the volume of which time I have seen
Hours dreadful and things strange; but this sore night
Hath trifled former knowings.

ROSS.

Ah, good father,
Thou seest, the heavens, as troubled with man's act,
Threatens his bloody stage: by the clock, 'tis day,
And yet dark night strangles the travelling lamp:
Is't night's predominance, or the day's shame,
That darkness does the face of earth entomb,
When living light should kiss it?

OLD MAN.

'Tis unnatural,
Even like the deed that's done. On Tuesday last,
A falcon, towering in her pride of place,

63

Was by a mousing owl hawk'd at and kill'd.

ROSS.

And Duncan's horses — a thing most strange
and certain —
Beauteous and swift, the minions of their
race,
Turn'd wild in nature, broke their stalls,
flung out,
Contending 'gainst obedience, as they would
make
War with mankind.

OLD MAN.

'Tis said they eat each other.

ROSS.

They did so, — to the amazement of mine
eyes
That look'd upon't. — Here comes the good
Macduff.

Enter MACDUFF.

How goes the world, sir, now?

MACDUFF.

Why, see you not?

ROSS.

Is't known who did this more than bloody
deed?

MACDUFF.

Those that Macbeth hath slain.

ROSS.

Alas, the day!
What good could they pretend?

MACDUFF.

They were suborn'd:
Malcolm and Donalbain, the king's two sons,
Are stol'n away and fled; which puts upon them
Suspicion of the deed.

ROSS.

'Gainst nature still!
Thriftless ambition, that wilt ravin up
Thine own life's means! — Then 'tis most like
The sovereignty will fall upon Macbeth.

MACDUFF.

He is already named, and gone to Scone
To be invested.

ROSS.

Where is Duncan's body?

MACDUFF.

Carried to Colmekill,
The sacred storehouse of his predecessors,
And guardian of their bones.

ROSS.

Will you to Scone?

MACDUFF.

No, cousin, I'll to Fife.

ROSS.

Well, I will thither.

MACDUFF.

Well, may you see things well done there,
— adieu, —
Lest our old robes sit easier than our new!

ROSS.

Farewell, father.

OLD MAN.
   God's benison go with you; and with those
That would make good of bad, and friends
of foes!

                                    [*Exeunt.*

ACT III

Scene I.

Forres. The palace.
Enter BANQUO.

BANQUO.
Thou hast it now, — king, Cawdor, Glamis, all,
As the weird women promised, and, I fear,
Thou play'dst most foully for't: yet it was said
It should not stand in thy posterity,
But that myself should be the root and father
Of many kings. If there come truth from
them —
As upon thee, Macbeth, their speeches
shine —
Why, by the verities on thee made good,
May they not be my oracles as well,
And set me up in hope? But hush! no more.

Sennet sounded. Enter MACBETH, *as king,*
LADY MACBETH, *as queen,* LENNOX, ROSS,
LORDS, LADIES, *and* ATTENDANTS.

MACBETH.
Here's our chief guest.
LADY MACBETH.
           If he had been forgotten,
It had been as a gap in our great feast,

And all-thing unbecoming.

MACBETH.

Tonight we hold a solemn supper sir,
And I'll request your presence.

BANQUO.

Let your highness
Command upon me; to the which my duties
Are with a most indissoluble tie
For ever knit.

MACBETH.

Ride you this afternoon?

BANQUO.

Ay, my good lord.

MACBETH.

We should have else desired your good
advice —
Which still hath been both grave and
prosperous —
In this day's council; but we'll take tomorrow.
Is't far you ride?

BANQUO.

As far, my lord, as will fill up the time
'Twixt this and supper: go not my horse the
better,
I must become a borrower of the night
For a dark hour or twain.

MACBETH.

Fail not our feast.

BANQUO.

My lord, I will not.

MACBETH.

We hear, our bloody cousins are bestow'd

In England and in Ireland, not confessing
Their cruel parricide, filling their hearers
With strange invention: but of that tomorrow,
When therewithal we shall have cause of
state
Craving us jointly. Hie you to horse: adieu,
Till you return at night. Goes Fleance with
you?
BANQUO.
Ay, my good lord: our time does call upon 's.
MACBETH.
I wish your horses swift and sure of foot;
And so I do commend you to their backs.
Farewell.
                                        [*Exit* BANQUO.
Let every man be master of his time
Till seven at night; to make society
The sweeter welcome, we will keep ourself
Till supper-time alone: while then, God be
with you!
[*Exeunt all but* MACBETH, *and an* ATTENDANT.
Sirrah, a word with you: attend those men
Our pleasure?
ATTENDANT.
They are, my lord, without the palace gate.
MACBETH.
Bring them before us.
                                [*Exit* ATTENDANT.
                        To be thus is nothing;
But to be safely thus. — Our fears in
Banquo
Stick deep; and in his royalty of nature

Reigns that which would be fear'd; 'tis much
he dares;
And, to that dauntless temper of his mind,
He hath a wisdom that doth guide his
valour
To act in safety. There is none but he
Whose being I do fear: and, under him,
My genius is rebuked; as, it is said,
Mark Antony's was by Caesar. He chid the
sisters
When first they put the name of king upon
me,
And bade them speak to him; then prophet-like
They hail'd him father to a line of kings:
Upon my head they placed a fruitless crown,
And put a barren sceptre in my gripe,
Thence to be wrench'd with an unlineal
hand,
No son of mine succeeding. If 't be so,
For Banquo's issue have I filed my mind;
For them the gracious Duncan have I
murder'd;
Put rancours in the vessel of my peace
Only for them; and mine eternal jewel
Given to the common enemy of man,
To make them kings, the seed of Banquo
kings!
Rather than so, come fate into the list.
And champion me to the utterance! — Who's
there!

Enter ATTENDANT, *with two* MURDERERS.

Now go to the door, and stay there till
we call.

[*Exit* ATTENDANT.

Was it not yesterday we spoke together?

FIRST MURDERER.

It was, so please your highness.

MACBETH.

Well then, now
Have you consider'd of my speeches? Know
That it was he in the times past which
held you
So under fortune; which you thought had
been
Our innocent self: this I made good to you
In our last conference, pass'd in probation
with you,
How you were borne in hand, how cross'd,
the instruments,
Who wrought with them, and all things else
that might
To half a soul and to a notion crazed
Say 'Thus did Banquo.'

FIRST MURDERER.

You made it known to us.

MACBETH.

I did so, and went further, which is now
Our point of second meeting. Do you find
Your patience so predominant in your nature
That you can let this go? Are you so gospell'd
To pray for this good man and for his issue,
Whose heavy hand hath bow'd you to the
grave

And beggar'd yours for ever?
FIRST MURDERER.

We are men, my liege.
MACBETH.
Ay, in the catalogue ye go for men;
As hounds and greyhounds, mongrels, spaniels, curs,
Shoughs, water-rugs and demi-wolves, are clept
All by the name of dogs: the valued file
Distinguishes the swift, the slow, the subtle,
The housekeeper, the hunter, every one
According to the gift which bounteous nature
Hath in him closed; whereby he does receive
Particular addition. from the bill
That writes them all alike: and so of men.
Now, if you have a station in the file,
Not i' the worst rank of manhood, say 't;
And I will put that business in your bosoms,
Whose execution takes your enemy off,
Grapples you to the heart and love of us,
Who wear our health but sickly in his life,
Which in his death were perfect.
SECOND MURDERER.

I am one, my liege,
Whom the vile blows and buffets of the world
Have so incensed that I am reckless what
I do to spite the world.
FIRST MURDERER.

And I another
So weary with disasters, tugg'd with fortune,

That I would set my life on any chance,
To mend it, or be rid on't.
MACBETH.
                              Both of you
Know Banquo was your enemy.
BOTH MURDERERS.
                              True, my lord.
MACBETH.
So is he mine; and in such bloody distance,
That every minute of his being thrusts
Against my near'st of life: and though I
could
With barefaced power sweep him from my
sight
And bid my will avouch it, yet I must not,
For certain friends that are both his and
mine,
Whose loves I may not drop, but wail his
fall
Who I myself struck down; and thence it is,
That I to your assistance do make love,
Masking the business from the common eye
For sundry weighty reasons.
SECOND MURDERER.
                              We shall, my lord,
Perform what you command us.
FIRST MURDERER.
                              Though our lives —
MACBETH.
Your spirits shine through you. Within this
hour at most
I will advise you where to plant yourselves;

75

Acquaint you with the perfect spy o' the
time,
The moment on't; for't must be done tonight,
And something from the palace; always
thought
That I require a clearness: and with him —
To leave no rubs nor botches in the work —
Fleance his son, that keeps him company,
Whose absence is no less material to me
Than is his father's, must embrace the fate
Of that dark hour. Resolve yourselves apart:
I'll come to you anon.

BOTH MURDERERS.

We are resolved, my lord.

MACBETH.

I'll call upon you straight: abide within.

[*Exeunt* MURDERERS.

It is concluded: — Banquo, thy soul's flight,
If it find heaven, must find it out tonight.

[*Exit.*

Scene II.

The palace.
Enter LADY MACBETH *and a* SERVANT.

LADY MACBETH.
  Is Banquo gone from court?
SERVANT.
  Ay, madam, but returns again tonight.
LADY MACBETH.
  Say to the king, I would attend his leisure
  For a few words.
SERVANT.
                    Madam, I will.
                                      [*Exit.*
LADY MACBETH.
                    Naught's had, all's spent,
  Where our desire is got without content:
  'Tis safer to be that which we destroy
  Than by destruction dwell in doubtful joy.

Enter MACBETH.

  How now, my lord! why do you keep alone,
  Of sorriest fancies your companions making,
  Using those thoughts which should indeed
  have died
  With them they think on? Things without all
  remedy

77

Should be without regard: what's done is
done.

MACBETH.

We have scorch'd the snake, not kill'd it:
She'll close and be herself, whilst our poor
malice
Remains in danger of her former tooth.
But let the frame of things disjoint, both the
worlds suffer,
Ere we will eat our meal in fear and sleep
In the affliction of these terrible dreams
That shake us nightly: better be with the
dead,
Whom we, to gain our peace, have sent to
peace,
Than on the torture of the mind to lie
In restless ecstasy. Duncan is in his grave;
After life's fitful fever he sleeps well;
Treason has done his worst: nor steel, nor
poison,
Malice domestic, foreign levy, nothing,
Can touch him further.

LADY MACBETH.

　　　　　　　　Come on; gentle my lord,
Sleek o'er your rugged looks; be bright and
jovial
Among your guests tonight.

MACBETH.

So shall I, love; and so, I pray, be you:
Let your remembrance apply to Banquo;
Present him eminence, both with eye and
tongue:

Unsafe the while, that we
Must lave our honours in these flattering streams,
And make our faces vizards to our hearts,
Disguising what they are.

LADY MACBETH.

                              You must leave this.

MACBETH.

O, full of scorpions is my mind, dear wife!
Thou know'st that Banquo, and his Fleance, lives.

LADY MACBETH.

But in them nature's copy's not eterne.

MACBETH.

There's comfort yet; they are assailable;
Then be thou jocund: ere the bat hath flown
His cloister'd flight, ere to black Hecate's summons
The shard-borne beetle with his drowsy hums
Hath rung night's yawning peal, there shall be done
A deed of dreadful note.

LADY MACBETH.

                              What's to be done?

MACBETH.

Be innocent of the knowledge, dearest chuck,
Till thou applaud the deed. — Come, seeling night,
Scarf up the tender eye of pitiful day;
And with thy bloody and invisible hand
Cancel and tear to pieces that great bond

Which keeps me pale! — Light thickens; and
the crow
Makes wing to the rooky wood:
Good things of day begin to droop and
drowse;
Whiles night's black agents to their preys do
rouse. —
Thou marvell'st at my words: but hold thee
still;
Things bad begun make strong themselves
by ill.
So, prithee, go with me.

[*Exeunt.*

Scene III.

A park, with a gate leading to the palace.
Enter three MURDERERS.

FIRST MURDERER.
  But who did bid thee join with us?
THIRD MURDERER.

                        Macbeth.

SECOND MURDERER.
  He needs not our mistrust, since he delivers
Our offices and what we have to do
To the direction just.
FIRST MURDERER.

                  Then stand with us.
The west yet glimmers with some streaks
of day:
Now spurs the lated traveller apace
To gain the timely inn; and near approaches
The subject of our watch.
THIRD MURDERER.

                 Hark! I hear horses.
BANQUO [*within*].
  Give us a light there, ho!
SECOND MUREDERER.

             Then 'tis he: the rest
That are within the note of expectation
Already are i' the court.

FIRST MURDERER.

His horses go about.

THIRD MURDERER.
Almost a mile: but he does usually,
So all men do, from hence to the palace
gate
Make it their walk.

SECOND MURDERER.

A light, a light!

THIRD MURDERER.

'Tis he.

FIRST MURDERER.
Stand to't.

Enter BANQUO, *and* FLEANCE *with a torch.*

BANQUO.
It will be rain tonight.

FIRST MURDERER.

Let it come down.
[*They assault* BANQUO.

BANQUO.
O, treachery! — Fly, good Fleance, fly, fly,
fly!
Thou mayst revenge. — O slave!
[*Dies.* FLEANCE *escapes.*

THIRD MURDERER.
Who did strike out the light?

FIRST MURDERER.

Was't not the way?

THIRD MURDERER.
There's but one down; the son is fled.

SECOND MURDERER.

We have lost

Best half of our affair.

FIRST MURDERER.

Well, let's away, and say how much is done.

[*Exeunt.*

Scene IV.

A room of state in the palace.
A banquet prepared. Enter MACBETH,
LADY MACBETH, ROSS, LENNOX,
LORDS, *and* ATTENDANTS.

MACBETH.

You know your own degrees, sit down: at
first

And last the hearty welcome.

LORDS.

Thanks to your majesty.

MACBETH.

Ourself will mingle with society,

And play the humble host.

Our hostess keeps her state, but in best time

We will require her welcome.

LADY MACBETH.

Pronounce it for me, sir, to all our friends;

For my heart speaks they are welcome.

MACBETH.

See, they encounter thee with their hearts'
thanks. —

Both sides are even: here I'll sit i' the midst:

Enter first MURDERER *to the door.*

85

Be large in mirth; anon we'll drink a measure
The table round: — There's blood upon
thy face.

FIRST MURDERER.

'Tis Banquo's then.

MACBETH.

'Tis better thee without than he within.
Is he dispatch'd?

FIRST MURDERER.

My lord, his throat is cut; that I did for
him.

MACBETH.

Thou art the best o' the cut-throats: yet
he's good
That did the like for Fleance: if thou didst
it,
Thou art the nonpareil.

FIRST MURDERER.

                                    Most royal sir,
Fleance is 'scaped.

MACBETH.

Then comes my fit again: I had else been
perfect,
Whole as the marble, founded as the rock;
As broad and general as the casing air:
But now I am cabin'd, cribb'd, confined,
bound in
To saucy doubts and fears. But Banquo's safe?

FIRST MURDERER.

Ay, my good lord: safe in a ditch he bides,
With twenty trenched gashes on his head;
The least a death to nature.

MACBETH.

Thanks for that:
There the grown serpent lies; the worm,
that's fled
Hath nature that in time will venom breed,
No teeth for the present. — Get thee gone:
tomorrow
We'll hear, ourselves, again.

[*Exit* MURDERER.

LADY MACBETH.

My royal lord,
You do not give the cheer: the feast is sold
That is not often vouch'd, while 'tis a-making,
'Tis given with welcome: to feed were best at
home;
From thence the sauce to meat is ceremony;
Meeting were bare without it.

MACBETH.

Sweet remembrancer! —
Now, good digestion wait on appetite,
And health on both!

LENNOX.

May't please your highness sit?

The GHOST OF BANQUO *enters,*
and sits in MACBETH'S *place.*

MACBETH.

Here had we now our country's honour
roof'd,
Were the graced person of our Banquo
present;

87

Who may I rather challenge for unkindness
Than pity for mischance!

ROSS.

His absence, sir,
Lays blame upon his promise. Please't your
highness
To grace us with your royal company?

MACBETH.

The table's full.

LENNOX.

Here is a place reserved, sir.

MACBETH.

Where?

LENNOX.

Here, my good lord. What is't that moves
your highness?

MACBETH.

Which of you have done this?

LORDS

What, my good lord?

MACBETH.

Thou canst not say I did it: never shake
Thy gory locks at me.

ROSS.

Gentlemen, rise: his highness is not well.

LADY MACBETH.

Sit, worthy friends: — my lord is often thus,
And hath been from his youth: pray you,
keep seat;
The fit is momentary; upon a thought
He will again be well: if much you note him,
You shall offend him and extend his passion:

Feed, and regard him not. — Are you a man?

MACBETH.

Ay, and a bold one, that dare look on that
Which might appal the devil.

LADY MACBETH.

O proper stuff!
This is the very painting of your fear:
This is the air-drawn dagger which, you said,
Led you to Duncan. O, these flaws and starts,
Impostors to true fear, would well become
A woman's story at a winter's fire,
Authorized by her grandam. Shame itself!
Why do you make such faces? When all's done,
You look but on a stool.

MACBETH.

Prithee, see there! behold! look! lo! how say you? —
Why, what care I? If thou canst nod, speak too. —
If charnel-houses and our graves must send
Those that we bury back, our monuments
Shall be the maws of kites.

[GHOST OF BANQUO *vanishes.*

LADY MACBETH.

What, quite unmann'd in folly?

MACBETH.

If I stand here, I saw him.

LADY MACBETH.

Fie, for shame!

MACBETH.

Blood hath been shed ere now, i' the olden time,
Ere human statute purged the gentle weal;
Ay, and since too, murders have been perform'd
Too terrible for the ear: the time has been,
That, when the brains were out, the man would die,
And there an end; but now they rise again,
With twenty mortal murders on their crowns,
And push us from our stools: this is more strange
Than such a murder is.

LADY MACBETH.

                   My worthy lord,
Your noble friends do lack you.

MACBETH.

                     I do forget: —
Do not muse at me, my most worthy friends,
I have a strange infirmity, which is nothing
To those that know me. Come, love and health to all;
Then I'll sit down. — Give me some wine; fill full.
I drink to the general joy o' the whole table,
And to our dear friend Banquo, whom we miss;
Would he were here! to all, and him, we thirst,
And all to all.

LORDS.

               Our duties, and the pledge.

Enter GHOST OF BANQUO.

MACBETH.

Avaunt! and quit my sight! let the earth
hide thee!
Thy bones are marrowless, thy blood is cold;
Thou hast no speculation in those eyes
Which thou dost glare with!

LADY MACBETH.

Think of this, good peers,
But as a thing of custom: 'tis no other;
Only it spoils the pleasure of the time.

MACBETH.

What man dare, I dare.
Approach thou like the rugged Russian bear,
The arm'd rhinoceros, or the Hyrcan tiger;
Take any shape but that, and my firm
nerves
Shall never tremble: or be alive again,
And dare me to the desert with thy sword;
If trembling I inhabit then, protest me
The baby of a girl. Hence, horrible shadow!
Unreal mockery, hence!

[GHOST OF BANQUO *vanishes.*

Why, so; — being gone,
I am a man again. — Pray you, sit still.

LADY MACBETH.

You have displaced the mirth, broke the good
meeting,
With most admired disorder.

MACBETH.

Can such things be,

91

And overcome us like a summer's cloud,
Without our special wonder? You make me
strange
Even to the disposition that I owe,
When now I think you can behold such
sights,
And keep the natural ruby of your cheeks,
When mine is blanch'd with fear.

ROSS.

What sights, my lord?

LADY MACBETH.

I pray you, speak not; he grows worse and
worse;
Question enrages him. At once, good night: —
Stand not upon the order of your going,
But go at once.

LENNOX.

Good night; and better health
Attend his majesty!

LADY MACBETH.

A kind good night to all!

[*Exeunt all but* MACBETH *and* LADY MACBETH.

MACBETH.

It will have blood; they say, blood will have
blood:
Stones have been known to move and trees
to speak;
Augurs and understood relations have
By maggot-pies and choughs and rooks
brought forth
The secret'st man of blood. — What is the
night?

LADY MACBETH.

Almost at odds with morning, which is which.

MACBETH.

How say'st thou, that Macduff denies his person

At our great bidding?

LADY MACBETH.

                              Did you send to him, sir?

MACBETH.

I hear it by the way; but I will send:

There's not a one of them but in his house

I keep a servant fee'd. I will tomorrow,

And betimes I will, to the weird sisters:

More shall they speak; for now I am bent to know,

By the worst means, the worst. For mine own good,

All causes shall give way: I am in blood

Stepp'd in so far that, should I wade no more,

Returning were as tedious as go o'er:

Strange things I have in head, that will to hand;

Which must be acted ere they may be scann'd.

LADY MACBETH.

You lack the season of all natures, sleep.

MACBETH.

Come, we'll to sleep. My strange and self-abuse

Is the initiate fear that wants hard use: —

We are yet but young in deed.   [*Exeunt.*

Scene V.

A Heath.
Thunder. Enter the three WITCHES,
meeting HECATE.

FIRST WITCH.
Why, how now, Hecate! you look angerly.
HECATE.
Have I not reason, beldams as you are,
Saucy and overbold? How did you dare
To trade and traffic with Macbeth
In riddles and affairs of death;
And I, the mistress of your charms,
The close contriver of all harms,
Was never call'd to bear my part,
Or show the glory of our art?
And, which is worse, all you have done
Hath been but for a wayward son,
Spiteful and wrathful, who, as others do,
Loves for his own ends, not for you.
But make amends now: get you gone,
And at the pit of Acheron
Meet me i' the morning: thither he
Will come to know his destiny:
Your vessels and your spells provide,
Your charms and every thing beside.
I am for the air; this night I'll spend

95

Unto a dismal and a fatal end:
Great business must be wrought ere noon:
Upon the corner of the moon
There hangs a vaporous drop profound;
I'll catch it ere it come to ground:
And that distill'd by magic sleights
Shall raise such artificial sprites
As by the strength of their illusion
Shall draw him on to his confusion:
He shall spurn fate, scorn death, and bear
He hopes 'bove wisdom, grace and fear:
And you all know, security
Is mortals' chiefest enemy.

> [*Music and a song within,* 'Come away,
> come away,' *&c.*

Hark! I am call'd; my little spirit, see,
Sits in a foggy cloud, and stays for me.

> [*Exit.*

FIRST WITCH.
Come, let's make haste; she'll soon be back
again.

> [*Exeunt.*

Scene VI.

Forres. A room in the palace.
Enter LENNOX *and another* LORD.

LENNOX.

My former speeches have but hit your
thoughts,
Which can interpret further: only, I say,
Things have been strangely borne. The
gracious Duncan
Was pitied of Macbeth: — marry, he was
dead: —
And the right-valiant Banquo walk'd too
late;
Whom, you may say, if't please you, Fleance
kill'd,
For Fleance fled: men must not walk too
late.
Who cannot want the thought how monstrous
It was for Malcolm and for Donalbain
To kill their gracious father? damned fact!
How it did grieve Macbeth! did he not
straight
In pious rage the two delinquents tear,
That were the slaves of drink and thralls of
sleep?
Was not that nobly done? Ay, and wisely too;

For 'twould have anger'd any heart alive
To hear the men deny't. So that, I say,
He has borne all things well: and I do think
That had he Duncan's sons under his key —
As, an't please heaven, he shall not — they
should find
What 'twere to kill a father; so should Fleance.
But, peace! — for from broad words and
'cause he fail'd
His presence at the tyrant's feast, I hear
Macduff lives in disgrace: sir, can you tell
Where he bestows himself?

LORD.
                     The son of Duncan,
From whom this tyrant holds the due of
birth
Lives in the English court, and is received
Of the most pious Edward with such grace
That the malevolence of fortune nothing
Takes from his high respect: thither Macduff
Is gone to pray the holy king, upon his aid
To wake Northumberland and warlike Siward:
That, by the help of these — with Him
above
To ratify the work — we may again
Give to our tables meat, sleep to our nights,
Free from our feasts and banquets bloody
knives,
Do faithful homage and receive free honours; —
All which we pine for now: and this report
Hath so exasperate their king that he
Prepares for some attempt of war.

LENNOX.

                              Sent he to Macduff?

LORD.

He did: and with an absolute 'Sir, not I,'
The cloudy messenger turns me his back,
And hums, as who should say, 'You'll rue
the time
That clogs me with this answer.'

LENNOX.

                              And that well might
Advise him to a caution, to hold what
distance
His wisdom can provide. Some holy angel
Fly to the court of England and unfold
His message ere he come; that a swift blessing
May soon return to this our suffering country
Under a hand accursed!

LORD.

                    I'll send my prayers with him.
                                        [Exeunt.

LENNOX

Sent he to Macduff?

LORD

He did: and with an absolute 'Sir, not I,'
  The cloudy messenger turns me his back,
And hums, as who should say 'You'll rue the time
  That clogs me with this answer.'

LENNOX

       And that well might
Advise him to a caution, to hold what distance
  His wisdom can provide. Some holy angel
    Fly to the court of England and unfold
His message ere he come, that a swift blessing
May soon return to this our suffering country
  Under a hand accursed!

LORD

I'll send my prayers with him.
Exeunt.

ACT IV

ACT IV

Scene I.

A cavern. In the middle, a cauldron boiling.
Thunder. Enter the three WITCHES.

FIRST WITCH.

Thrice the brinded cat hath mew'd.

SECOND WITCH.

Thrice and once the hedge-pig whined.

THIRD WITCH.

Harpier cries: — 'Tis time, 'tis time.

FIRST WITCH.

Round about the cauldron go;
In the poison'd entrails throw.
Toad, that under cold stone
Days and nights has thirty-one
Swelter'd venom sleeping got,
Boil thou first i' the charmed pot.

ALL.

Double, double toil and trouble;
Fire burn, and cauldron bubble.

SECOND WITCH.

Fillet of a fenny snake,
In the cauldron boil and bake;
Eye of newt and toe of frog,
Wool of bat and tongue of dog,
Adder's fork and blind-worm's sting,
Lizard's leg and owlet's wing, —

For a charm of powerful trouble,
Like a hell-broth boil and bubble.

ALL.

Double, double toil and trouble;
Fire burn and cauldron bubble.

THIRD WITCH.

Scale of dragon, tooth of wolf,
Witches' mummy, maw and gulf
Of the ravin'd salt-sea shark,
Root of hemlock digg'd i' the dark,
Liver of blaspheming Jew,
Gall of goat, and slips of yew
Silver'd in the moon's eclipse,
Nose of Turk and Tartar's lips,
Finger of birth-strangled babe
Ditch-deliver'd by a drab, —
Make the gruel thick and slab:
Add thereto a tiger's chaudron,
For the ingredients of our cauldron.

ALL.

Double, double toil and trouble;
Fire burn and cauldron bubble.

SECOND WITCH.

Cool it with a baboon's blood,
Then the charm is firm and good.

Enter HECATE *to the other three* WITCHES.

HECATE.

O well done! I commend your pains;
And every one shall share i' the gains;
And now about the cauldron sing,

Live elves and fairies in a ring,
Enchanting all that you put in.
[*Music and a song:* 'Black spirits,' *&c.*
[*Exit* HECATE.

SECOND WITCH.
By the pricking of my thumbs,
Something wicked this way comes: —
Open, locks,
Whoever knocks!

Enter MACBETH.

MACBETH.
How now, you secret, black, and midnight
hags!
What is't you do?

ALL.
                          A deed without a name.

MACBETH.
I conjure you, by that which you profess, —
Howe'er you come to know it, — answer me:
Though you untie the winds and let them
fight
Against the churches; though the yesty waves
Confound and swallow navigation up;
Though bladed corn be lodged and trees
blown down;
Though castles topple on their warders' heads;
Though palaces and pyramids do slope
Their heads to their foundations; though the
treasure
Of nature's germens tumble all together,

Even till destruction sicken; — answer me
To what I ask you.
FIRST WITCH.

                    Speak.

SECOND WITCH.

                      Demand.

THIRD WITCH.

                      We'll answer.

FIRST WITCH.
Say, if thou'dst rather hear it from our
mouths,
Or from our masters?
MACBETH.

                Call 'em; let me see 'em.

FIRST WITCH.
Pour in sow's blood, that hath eaten
Her nine farrow; grease that's sweaten
From the murderer's gibbet throw
Into the flame.
ALL.

            Come, high or low;
          Thyself and office deftly show!

Thunder. FIRST APPARITION: *an armed Head.*

MACBETH.
Tell me, thou unknown power, —
FIRST WITCH.

              He knows thy thought:
Hear his speech, but say thou naught.
FIRST APPARITION.
Macbeth! Macbeth! Macbeth! beware Macduff;

Beware the thane of Fife. — Dismiss me:
— enough.

> [*Descends.*

MACBETH.

Whate'er thou art, for thy good caution,
thanks;
Thou hast harp'd my fear aright: — but one
word more, —

FIRST WITCH.

He will not be commanded: here's another,
More potent than the first.

Thunder. SECOND APPARITION: *A bloody Child.*

SECOND APPARITION.

Macbeth! Macbeth! Macbeth! —

MACBETH.

Had I three ears, I'd hear thee.

SECOND APPARITION.

Be bloody, bold, and resolute; laugh to scorn
The power of man, for none of woman born
Shall harm Macbeth.

> [*Descends.*

MACBETH.

Then live, Macduff: what need I fear of
thee?
But yet I'll make assurance double sure,
And take a bond of fate: thou shalt not live;
That I may tell pale-hearted fear it lies,
And sleep in spite of thunder.

Thunder. THIRD APPARITION: *a Child crowned, with a tree in his hand.*

What is this
That rises like the issue of a king,
And wears upon his baby-brow the round
And top of sovereignty?

ALL.

Listen, but speak not to't.

THIRD APPARITION.

Be lion-mettled, proud; and take no care
Who chafes, who frets, or where conspirers
are:
Macbeth shall never vanquish'd be until
Great Birnam wood to high Dunsinane hill
Shall come against him.

[*Descends.*

MACBETH.

That will never be:
Who can impress the forest, bid the tree
Unfix his earth-bound root? Sweet bodements!
good!
Rebellious dead, rise never till the wood
Of Birnam rise, and our high-placed Macbeth
Shall live the lease of nature, pay his breath
To time and mortal custom. — Yet my
heart
Throbs to know one thing: tell me, — if
your art
Can tell so much, — shall Banquo's issue
ever
Reign in this kingdom?

ALL.

                                    Seek to know no more.

MACBETH.

I will be satisfied: deny me this,
And an eternal curse fall on you! Let me
know: —
Why sinks that cauldron? and what noise
is this?

                                              [*Hautboys.*

FIRST WITCH.

Show!

SECOND WITCH.

Show!

THIRD WITCH.

Show!

ALL.

Show his eyes, and grieve his heart;
Come like shadows, so depart!

A show of Eight KINGS, *the last with a glass
in his hand;* GHOST OF BANQUO *following.*

MACBETH.

Thou art too like the spirit of Banquo:
down!
Thy crown does sear mine eye-balls: — and
thy hair,
Thou other gold-bound brow, is like the
first: —
A third is like the former. — Filthy hags!
Why do you show me this? — A fourth!
— Start, eyes! —

What, will the line stretch out to the crack of
doom? —
Another yet! — A seventh! — I'll see no
more: —
And yet the eighth appears, who bears a
glass
Which shows me many more; and some I
see
That two-fold balls and treble sceptres carry:
Horrible sight! — Now, I see, 'tis true;
For the blood-bolter'd Banquo smiles upon
me,
And points at them for his.

                              [*Apparitions vanish.*
What, is this so?

FIRST WITCH.
Ay, sir, all this is so: — but why
Stands Macbeth thus amazedly? —
Come, sisters, cheer we up his sprites,
And show the best of our delights:
I'll charm the air to give a sound,
While you perform your antic round;
That this great king may kindly say,
Our duties did his welcome pay.

[*Music. The* WITCHES *dance and then vanish.*

MACBETH.
Where are they? Gone? — Let this pernicious
hour
Stand aye accursed in the calendar! —
Come in, without there!

Enter LENNOX.

110

LENNOX.

What's your grace's will?

MACBETH.

Saw you the weird sisters?

LENNOX.

No, my lord.

MACBETH.

Came they not by you?

LENNOX.

No, indeed, my lord.

MACBETH.

Infected be the air whereon they ride;
And damn'd all those that trust them! — I did hear
The galloping of horse: who was't came by?

LENNOX.

'Tis two or three, my lord, that bring you word
Macduff is fled to England.

MACBETH.

Fled to England!

LENNOX.

Ay, my good lord.

MACBETH.

Time, thou anticipatest my dread exploits:
The flighty purpose never is o'ertook
Unless the deed go with it; from this moment
The very firstlings of my heart shall be
The firstlings of my hand. And even now,
To crown my thoughts with acts, be it thought
and done:
The castle of Macduff I will surprise;

Seize upon Fife; give to the edge o' the
sword
His wife, his babes, and all unfortunate souls
That trace him in his line. No boasting like
a fool;
This deed I'll do before this purpose cool.
But no more sights! — Where are these
gentlemen?
Come, bring me where they are.
[*Exeunt.*

Scene II.

Fife. A room in MACDUFF'S castle.
Enter LADY MACDUFF, *her* SON, *and* ROSS.

LADY MACDUFF.
What had he done, to make him fly the land?
ROSS.
You must have patience, madam.
LADY MACDUFF.

                   He had none:
His flight was madness: when our actions
do not,
Our fears do make us traitors.
ROSS.

                   You know not
Whether it was his wisdom or his fear.
LADY MACDUFF.
Wisdom! to leave his wife, to leave his
babes,
His mansion and his titles in a place
From whence himself does fly? He loves
us not;
He wants the natural touch: for the poor
wren,
The most diminutive of birds, will fight,
Her young ones in her nest, against the owl.
All is the fear and nothing is the love;

As little is the wisdom, where the flight
So runs against all reason.

ROSS.

                                My dearest coz,
I pray you, school yourself: but for your
husband,
He is noble, wise, judicious, and best knows
The fits o' the season. I dare not speak much
further;
But cruel are the times, when we are traitors
And do not know ourselves; when we hold
rumour
From what we fear, yet know not what
we fear,
But float upon a wild and violent sea
Each way and move. — I take my leave
of you:
Shall not be long but I'll be here again:
Things at the worst will cease, or else climb
upward
To what they were before. — My pretty
cousin,
Blessing upon you!

LADY MACDUFF.

Father'd he is, and yet he's fatherless.

ROSS.

I am so much a fool, should I stay longer,
It would be my disgrace and your discomfort:
I take my leave at once.

                                      [*Exit.*

LADY MACDUFF.

                         Sirrah, your father's dead;

And what will you do now? How will you
live?

SON.

As birds do, mother.

LADY MACDUFF.

What, with worms and flies?

SON.

With what I get, I mean; and so do they.

LADY MACDUFF.

Poor bird! thou'ldst never fear the net nor lime,
The pitfall nor the gin.

SON.

Why should I, mother? Poor birds they are
not set for.
My father is not dead, for all your saying.

LADY MACDUFF.

Yes, he is dead; how wilt thou do for a
father?

SON.

Nay, how will you do for a husband?

LADY MACDUFF.

Why, I can buy me twenty at any market.

SON.

Then you'll buy 'em to sell again.

LADY MACDUFF.

Thou speak'st with all thy wit; and yet,
i' faith,
With wit enough for thee.

SON.

Was my father a traitor, mother?

LADY MACDUFF.

Ay, that he was.

SON.
  What is a traitor?

LADY MACDUFF.
  Why, one that swears and lies.

SON.
  And be all traitors that do so?

LADY MACDUFF.
  Every one that does so is a traitor, and must be hanged.

SON.
  And must they all be hanged that swear and lie?

LADY MACDUFF.
  Every one.

SON.
  Who must hang them?

LADY MACDUFF.
  Why, the honest men.

SON.
  Then the liars and swearers are fools, for there are liars and swearers enow to beat the honest men and hang up them.

LADY MACDUFF.
  Now, God help thee, poor monkey!
  But how wilt thou do for a father?

SON.
  If he were dead, you'd weep for him: if you would not, it were a good sign that I should quickly have a new father.

LADY MACDUFF.
  Poor prattler, how thou talk'st!

Enter a MESSENGER.

MESSENGER.
Bless you, fair dame! I am not to you
known,
Though in your state of honour I am perfect.
I doubt some danger does approach you
nearly:
If you will take a homely man's advice,
Be not found here; hence, with your little
ones.
To fright you thus, methinks, I am too
savage;
To do worse to you were fell cruelty,
Which is too nigh your person. Heaven
preserve you!
I dare abide no longer.
                                              [*Exit.*
LADY MACDUFF.
                    Whither should I fly?
I have done no harm. But I remember now
I am in this earthly world; where to do harm
Is often laudable, to do good, sometime
Accounted dangerous folly: why then, alas,
Do I put up that womanly defence,
To say I have done no harm?

Enter MURDERERS.

                    What are these faces?
FIRST MURDERER.
Where is your husband?

LADY MACDUFF.
　I hope, in no place so unsanctified
　Where such as thou mayst find him.
FIRST MURDERER.
　　　　　　　　　　　　　　He's a traitor.
SON.
　Thou liest, thou shag-hair'd villain!
FIRST MURDERER.
　What, you egg!　　　　　　　　[*Stabbing him.*
　Young fry of treachery!
SON.
　　　　　　　　He has kill'd me, mother:
　Run away, I pray you!
　　　　　　　　　　　　　　　　[*Dies.*
　[*Exit* LADY MACDUFF, *crying 'Murder!' and
　　pursued by the* MURDERERS.

Scene III.

England. Before the KING'S palace.
Enter MALCOLM *and* MACDUFF.

MALCOLM.

Let us seek out some desolate shade, and there
Weep our sad bosoms empty.

MACDUFF.

Let us rather
Hold fast the mortal sword, and like good men
Bestride our down-fall'n birthdom: each new morn
New widows howl, new orphans cry, new sorrows
Strike heaven on the face, that it resounds
As if it felt with Scotland, and yell'd out
Like syllable of dolour.

MALCOLM.

What I believe I'll wail;
What know, believe, and what I can, redress;
As I shall find the time to friend, I will.
What you have spoke, it may be so perchance.
This tyrant, whose sole name blisters our tongues,
Was once thought honest: you have loved him well.

He hath not touch'd you yet. I am young; but
something
You may deserve of him through me, and
wisdom
To offer up a weak poor innocent lamb
To appease an angry god.

MACDUFF.
I am not treacherous.

MALCOLM.

But Macbeth is.
A good and virtuous nature may recoil
In an imperial charge. But I shall crave your
pardon;
That which you are, my thoughts cannot
transpose:
Angels are bright still, though the brightest
fell;
Though all things foul would wear the brows
of grace,
Yet grace must still look so.

MACDUFF.
I have lost my hopes.

MALCOLM.
Perchance even there where I did find my
doubts.
Why in that rawness left you wife and child,
Those precious motives, those strong knots
of love,
Without leave-taking? — I pray you,
Let not my jealousies be your dishonours,
But mine own safeties: —you may be rightly
just,

Whatever I shall think.
MACDUFF.

Bleed, bleed, poor country!
Great tyranny! lay thou thy basis sure,
For goodness dare not check thee! wear thou
thy wrongs;
The title is affeer'd! — Fare thee well, lord:
I would not be the villain that thou think'st
For the whole space that's in the tyrant's
grasp,
And the rich East to boot.
MALCOLM.

Be not offended:
I speak not as in absolute fear of you.
I think our country sinks beneath the yoke;
It weeps, it bleeds; and each new day a gash
Is added to her wounds: I think withal
There would be hands uplifted in my right;
And here from gracious England have I offer
Of goodly thousands: but, for all this,
When I shall tread upon the tyrant's head,
Or wear it on my sword, yet my poor
country
Shall have more vices than it had before,
More suffer and more sundry ways than
ever,
By him that shall succeed.
MACDUFF.

What should he be?
MALCOLM.
It is myself I mean: in whom I know
All the particulars of vice so grafted

That, when they shall be open'd, black
Macbeth
Will seem as pure as snow, and the poor state
Esteem him as a lamb, being compared
With my confineless harms.
MACDUFF.

                     Not in the legions
Of horrid hell can come a devil more damn'd
In evils to top Macbeth.
MALCOLM.

               I grant him bloody,
Luxurious, avaricious, false, deceitful,
Sudden, malicious, smacking of every sin
That has a name: but there's no bottom,
none,
In my voluptuousness: your wives, your
daughters,
Your matrons and your maids, could not
fill up
The cistern of my lust, and my desire
All continent impediments would o'erbear
That did oppose my will: better Macbeth
Than such an one to reign.
MACDUFF.

                 Boundless intemperance
In nature is a tyranny; it hath been
The untimely emptying of the happy throne
And fall of many kings. But fear not yet
To take upon you what is yours.: you may
Convey your pleasures in a spacious plenty,
And yet seem cold, the time you may so
hoodwink.

We have willing dames enough; there cannot
be
That vulture in you, to devour so many
As will to greatness dedicate themselves,
Finding it so inclined.

MALCOLM.

                                   With this there grows
In my most ill-composed affection such
A stanchless avarice that, were I king,
I should cut off the nobles for their lands,
Desire his jewels and this other's house:
And my more-having would be as a sauce
To make me hunger more; that I should
forge
Quarrels unjust against the good and loyal,
Destroying them for wealth.

MACDUFF.

                                      This avarice
Sticks deeper, grows with more pernicious
root
Than summer-seeming lust, and it hath been
The sword of our slain kings: yet do not
fear;
Scotland hath foisons to fill up your will,
Of your mere own: all these are portable,
With other graces weigh'd.

MALCOLM.

But I have none: the king-becoming graces,
As justice, verity, temperance, stableness,
Bounty, perseverance, mercy, lowliness,
Devotion, patience, courage, fortitude,
I have no relish of them, but abound

In the division of each several crime,
Acting it many ways. Nay, had I power, I
should
Pour the sweet milk of concord into hell,
Uproar the universal peace, confound
All unity on earth.
MACDUFF.
                              O Scotland, Scotland!
MALCOLM.
If such a one be fit to govern, speak:
I am as I have spoken.
MACDUFF.
                                   Fit to govern!
No, not to live. — O nation miserable,
With an untitled tyrant bloody-sceptre'd,
When shalt thou see thy wholesome days
again,
Since that the truest issue of thy throne
By his own interdiction stands accursed,
And does blaspheme his breed? — Thy royal
father
Was a most sainted king: the queen that
bore thee,
Oftener upon her knees than on her feet,
Died every day she lived. Fare thee well!
These evils thou repeat'st upon thyself
Have banish'd me from Scotland. — O my
breast,
Thy hope ends here!
MALCOLM.
                         Macduff, this noble passion,
Child of integrity, hath from my soul

Wiped the black scruples, reconciled my
thoughts
To thy good truth and honour. Devilish
Macbeth
By many of these trains hath sought to win
me
Into his power, and modest wisdom plucks
me
From over-credulous haste: but God above
Deal between thee and me! for even now
I put myself to thy direction, and
Unspeak mine own detraction, here abjure
The taints and blames I laid upon myself,
For strangers to my nature. I am yet
Unknown to woman, never was forsworn,
Scarcely have coveted what was mine own,
At no time broke my faith, would not betray
The devil to his fellow and delight
No less in truth than life: my first false
speaking
Was this upon myself: — what I am truly,
Is thine and my poor country's to command: —
Whither indeed, before thy here-approach,
Old Siward, with ten thousand warlike men,
Already at a point, was setting forth.
Now we'll together; and the chance of
goodness
Be like our warranted quarrel! Why are you
silent?

MACDUFF.

Such welcome and unwelcome things at once
'Tis hard to reconcile.

Enter a DOCTOR.

MALCOLM.
Well; more anon. — Comes the king forth, I
pray you?
DOCTOR.
Ay, sir; there are a crew of wretched souls
That stay his cure: their malady convinces
The great assay of art; but at his touch,
Such sanctity hath heaven given his hand,
They presently amend.
MALCOLM.
                                    I thank you, doctor.
                                    [*Exit* DOCTOR.
MACDUFF.
What's the disease he means?
MALCOLM.
                                    'Tis call'd the evil:
A most miraculous work in this good king;
Which often, since my here-remain in England,
I have seen him do. How he solicits heaven,
Himself best knows: but strangely-visited
people,
All swoll'n and ulcerous, pitiful to the eye,
The mere despair of surgery, he cures,
Hanging a golden stamp about their necks,
Put on with holy prayers: and 'tis spoken,
To the succeeding royalty he leaves
The healing benediction. With this strange
virtue,
He hath a heavenly gift of prophecy,
And sundry blessings hang about his throne,

That speak him full of grace.

Enter ROSS.

MACDUFF.

See, who comes here?

MALCOLM.

My countryman; but yet I know him not.

MACDUFF.

My ever-gentle cousin, welcome hither.

MALCOLM.

I know him now: — good God, betimes remove

The means that makes us strangers!

ROSS.

Sir, amen.

MACDUFF.

Stands Scotland where it did?

ROSS.

Alas, poor country, —

Almost afraid to know itself. It cannot

Be call'd our mother, but our grave; where nothing,

But who knows nothing, is once seen to smile;

Where sighs and groans and shrieks that rend the air

Are made, not mark'd; where violent sorrow seems

A modern ecstasy; the dead man's knell

Is there scarce ask'd for who; and good men's lives

Expire before the flowers in their caps,
Dying or ere they sicken.
MACDUFF.

O, relation

Too nice, and yet too true!
MALCOLM.

What's the newest grief?

ROSS.
That of an hour's age doth hiss the speaker:
Each minute teems a new one.
MACDUFF.

How does my wife?

ROSS.
Why, well.
MACDUFF.

And all my children?

ROSS.

Well too.

MACDUFF.
The tyrant has not batter'd at their peace?
ROSS.
No; they were well at peace when I did
leave 'em.
MACDUFF.
Be not a niggard of your speech: how goes't?
ROSS.
When I came hither to transport the tidings,
Which I have heavily borne, there ran a
rumour
Of many worthy fellows that were out;
Which was to my belief witness'd the rather,
For that I saw the tyrant's power a-foot:

Now is the time of help; your eye in Scotland
Would create soldiers, make our women fight,
To doff their dire distresses.
MALCOLM.

                        Be't their comfort
We are coming thither: gracious England
hath
Lent us good Siward and ten thousand men;
An older and a better soldier none
That Christendom gives out.
ROSS.

                     Would I could answer
This comfort with the like! But I have words
That would be howl'd out in the desert air,
Where hearing should not latch them.
MACDUFF.

                      What concern they?
The general cause? or is it a fee-grief
Due to some single breast?
ROSS.

                    No mind that's honest
But in it shares some woe; though the main
part
Pertains to you alone.
MACDUFF.

                       If it be mine,
Keep it not from me, quickly let me have it.
ROSS.
Let not your ears despise my tongue for
ever,
Which shall possess them with the heaviest
sound

That ever yet they heard.

MACDUFF.

Hum! I guess at it.

ROSS.

Your castle is surprised; your wife and babes
Savagely slaughter'd: to relate the manner,
Were, on the quarry of these murder'd deer,
To add the death of you.

MALCOLM.

Merciful heaven! —
What, man! ne'er pull your hat upon your
brows;
Give sorrow words: the grief that does not
speak
Whispers the o'er-fraught heart and bids it
break.

MACDUFF.

My children too?

ROSS.

Wife, children, servants, all
That could be found.

MACDUFF.

And I must be from thence! —
My wife kill'd too?

ROSS.

I have said.

MALCOLM.

Be comforted:
Let's make us medicines of our great revenge,
To cure this deadly grief.

MACDUFF.

He has no children. — All my pretty ones?

130

Did you say all? — O hell-kite! —All?
What, all my pretty chickens and their dam
At one fell swoop?

MALCOLM.

Dispute it like a man.

MACDUFF.

                          I shall do so;
But I must also feel it as a man:
I cannot but remember such things were,
That were most precious to me. — Did heaven
look on,
And would not take their part? Sinful
Macduff,
They were all struck for thee! Naught that I
am,
Not for their own demerits, but for mine,
Fell slaughter on their souls. Heaven rest
them now!

MALCOLM.

Be this the whetstone of your sword: let
grief
Convert to anger; blunt not the heart, enrage
it.

MACDUFF.

O, I could play the woman with mine eyes
And braggart with my tongue! — But, gentle
heavens,
Cut short all intermission; front to front
Bring thou this fiend of Scotland and myself;
Within my sword's length set him; if he
'scape,
Heaven forgive him too!

MALCOLM.

                     This tune goes manly.
Come, go we to the king; our power is
ready;
Our lack is nothing but our leave; Macbeth
Is ripe for shaking, and the powers above
Put on their instruments. Receive what cheer
you may:
The night is long that never finds the day.
                                    [*Exeunt.*

ACT V

ACT V

Scene I.

Dunsinane. A room in the castle.
Enter a DOCTOR OF PHYSIC
and a WAITING-GENTLEWOMAN.

DOCTOR.

I have two nights watched with you, but can perceive no truth in your report. When was it she last walked?

GENTLEWOMAN.

Since his majesty went into the field, I have seen her rise from her bed, throw her night-gown upon her, unlock her closet, take forth paper, fold it, write upon't, read it, afterwards seal it, and again return to bed; yet all this while in a most fast sleep.

DOCTOR.

A great perturbation in nature, — to receive at once the benefit of sleep, and do the effects of watching! — In this slumbery agitation, besides her walking and other actual performances, what, at any time, have you heard her say?

GENTLEWOMAN.

That, sir, which I will not report after her.

DOCTOR.

You may to me; and 'tis most meet you should.

GENTLEWOMAN.

Neither to you nor any one; having no witness to confirm my speech. — Lo you, here she comes!

Enter LADY MACBETH, *with a taper.*

This is her very guise; and, upon my life, fast asleep.
Observe her; stand close.

DOCTOR.

How came she by that light?

GENTLEWOMAN.

Why, it stood by her: she has light by her continually; 'tis her command.

DOCTOR.

You see, her eyes are open.

GENTLEWOMAN.

Ay, but their sense are shut.

DOCTOR.

What is it she does now? Look, how she rubs her hands.

GENTLEWOMAN.

It is an accustomed action with her, to seem thus washing her hands: I have known her continue in this a quarter of an hour.

LADY MACBETH.

Yet here's a spot.

DOCTOR.

Hark! she speaks: I will set down what comes from her, to satisfy my remembrance the more strongly.

136

LADY MACBETH.

Out, damned spot! out, I say! — One, two;
why, then, 'tis time to do't. — Hell is murky!
— Fie, my lord, fie! a soldier, and afeard?
What need we fear who knows it, when none
can call our power to account? — Yet who
would have thought the old man to have had
so much blood in him?.

DOCTOR.

Do you mark that?

LADY MACBETH.

The thane of Fife had a wife; where is she
now? — What, will these hands ne'er be clean?
— No more o' that, my lord, no more o' that:
you mar all with this starting.

DOCTOR.

Go to, go to; you have known what you
should not.

GENTLEWOMAN.

She has spoke what she should not, I am
sure of that: heaven knows what she has
known.

LADY MACBETH.

Here's the smell of the blood still: all the
perfumes of Arabia will not sweeten this little
hand. Oh, oh, oh!

DOCTOR.

What a sigh is there! The heart is sorely
charged.

GENTLEWOMAN.

I would not have such a heart in my bosom
for the dignity of the whole body.

DOCTOR.

Well, well, well, —

GENTLEWOMAN.

Pray God it be, sir.

DOCTOR.

This disease is beyond my practice: yet I have
known those which have walked in their sleep
who have died holily in their beds.

LADY MACBETH.

Wash your hands, put on your nightgown;
look not so pale. — I tell you yet again,
Banquo's buried; he cannot come out on's
grave.

DOCTOR.

Even so?

LADY MACBETH.

To bed, to bed! there's knocking at the gate:
come, come, come, come, give me your hand.
What's done cannot be undone. — To bed, to
bed, to bed!

[*Exit.*

DOCTOR.

Will she go now to bed?

GENTLEWOMAN.

Directly.

DOCTOR.

Foul whisperings are abroad: unnatural deeds
Do breed unnatural troubles: infected minds
To their deaf pillows will discharge their
secrets:
More needs she the divine than the physician: —
God, God forgive us all! — Look after her;

Remove from her the means of all annoyance,
And still keep eyes upon her. — so, good night:
My mind she has mated, and amazed my sight:
I think, but dare not speak.
GENTLEWOMAN.

Good night, good doctor.
                                    [*Exeunt.*

Scene II.

The country near Dunsinane.
Drum and colours. Enter MENTEITH,
CAITHNESS, ANGUS, LENNOX, *and* SOLDIERS.

MENTEITH.
The English power is near, led on by
Malcolm,
His uncle Siward and the good Macduff:
Revenges burn in them; for their dear causes
Would to the bleeding and the grim alarm
Excite the mortified man.

ANGUS.
                              Near Birnam wood
Shall we well meet them; that way are they
coming.

CAITHNESS.
Who knows if Donalbain be with his brother?

LENNOX.
For certain, sir, he is not: I have a file
Of all the gentry: there is Siward's son,
And many unrough youths that even now
Protest their first of manhood.

MENTEITH.
                              What does the tyrant?

CAITHNESS.
Great Dunsinane he strongly fortifies:

141

Some say he's mad; others that lesser hate him
Do call it valiant fury: but, for certain,
He cannot buckle his distemper'd cause
Within the belt of rule.

ANGUS.

Now does he feel
His secret murders sticking on his hands;
Now minutely revolts upbraid his faith-breach;
Those he commands move only in command,
Nothing in love: now does he feel his title
Hang loose about him, like a giant's robe
Upon a dwarfish thief.

MENTEITH.

Who then shall blame
His pester'd senses to recoil and start,
When all that is within him does condemn
Itself for being there?

CAITHNESS.

Well, march we on,
To give obedience where 'tis truly owed:
Meet we the medicine of the sickly weal,
And with him pour we in our country's purge
Each drop of us.

LENNOX.

Or so much as it needs,
To dew the sovereign flower and drown the weeds.
Make we our march towards Birnam.

[*Exeunt, marching.*

142

Scene III.

Dunsinane. A room in the castle.
Enter MACBETH, DOCTOR, *and* ATTENDANTS.

MACBETH.
Bring me no more reports; let them fly all:
Till Birnam wood remove to Dunsinane,
I cannot taint with fear. What's the boy
Malcolm?
Was he not born of woman? The spirits
that know
All mortal consequences have pronounced
me thus:
'Fear not, Macbeth; no man that's born of
woman
Shall e'er have power upon thee.' — Then
fly, false thanes,
And mingle with the English epicures:
The mind I sway by and the heart I bear
Shall never sag with doubt nor shake with
fear.

Enter a SERVANT.

The devil damn thee black, thou cream-faced
loon!
Where got'st thou that goose look?

143

SERVANT.
There is ten thousand —
MACBETH.
                              Geese, villain?
SERVANT.
                              Soldiers, sir.
MACBETH.
Go prick thy face, and over-red thy fear,
Thou lily-liver'd boy. What soldiers, patch?
Death of thy soul! those linen cheeks of thine
Are counsellors to fear. What soldiers,
whey-face?
SERVANT.
The English force, so please you.
MACBETH.
Take thy face hence.
                              [*Exit* SERVANT.
                    Seyton! — I am sick at heart,
When I behold — Seyton, I say! — This push
Will cheer me ever, or disseat me now.
I have lived long enough: my way of life
Is fall'n into the seare, the yellow leaf;
And that which should accompany old age,
As honour, love, obedience, troops of friends,
I must not look to have; but, in their stead,
Curses, not loud but deep, mouth-honour,
breath,
Which the poor heart would fain deny, and
dare not.
Seyton!

                    Enter SEYTON.

SEYTON.
What is your gracious pleasure?
MACBETH.
                              What news more?
SEYTON.
All is confirm'd, my lord, which was reported.
MACBETH.
I'll fight till from my bones my flesh be hack'd.
Give me my armour.
SEYTON.
                              'Tis not needed yet.
MACBETH.
I'll put it on. —
Send out more horses; skirr the country round;
Hang those that talk of fear. — Give me mine armour. —
How does your patient, doctor?
DOCTOR.
                              Not so sick, my lord,
As she is troubled with thick coming fancies,
That keep her from her rest.
MACBETH.
                              Cure her of that.
Canst thou not minister to a mind diseased,
Pluck from the memory a rooted sorrow,
Raze out the written troubles of the brain
And with some sweet oblivious antidote
Cleanse the stuff'd bosom of that perilous stuff
Which weighs upon the heart?

145

DOCTOR.

                     Therein the patient
Must minister to himself.

MACBETH.

Throw physic to the dogs; — I'll none of
it. —
Come, put mine armour on; give me my
staff: —
Seyton, send out. — Doctor, the thanes fly
from me. —
Come, sir, dispatch. — If thou couldst,
doctor, cast
The water of my land, find her disease,
And purge it to a sound and pristine health,
I would applaud thee to the very echo,
That should applaud again. — Pull't off, I
say. —
What rhubarb, cyme, or what purgative drug,
Would scour these English hence? Hear'st
thou of them?

Doctor.

Ay, my good lord; your royal preparation
Makes us hear something.

MACBETH.

                    Bring it after me. —
I will not be afraid of death and bane,
Till Birnam forest come to Dunsinane.

                    [*Exeunt all but* DOCTOR.

DOCTOR [*aside*].

Were I from Dunsinane away and clear,
Profit again should hardly draw me here.

                            [*Exit.*

Scene IV.

Country near Dunsinane: a wood in view.
Drum and colours. Enter MALCOLM,
SIWARD *and* YOUNG SIWARD, MACDUFF,
MENTEITH, CAITHNESS, ANGUS, LENNOX,
ROSS, *and* SOLDIERS, *marching.*

MALCOLM.
  Cousins, I hope the days are near at hand
  That chambers will be safe.
MENTEITH.
                    We doubt it nothing.
SIWARD.
  What wood is this before us?
MENTEITH.
                    The wood of Birnam.
MALCOLM.
  Let every soldier hew him down a bough
  And bear't before him: thereby shall we
  shadow
  The numbers of our host and make discovery
  Err in report of us.
SOLDIER.
                    It shall be done.
SIWARD.
  We learn no other but the confident tyrant
  Keeps still in Dunsinane, and will endure

Our setting down before 't.

MALCOLM.

'Tis his main hope:
For where there is advantage to be given,
Both more and less have given him the
revolt,
And none serve with him but constrained
things
Whose hearts are absent too.

MACDUFF.

Let our just censures
Attend the true event, and put we on
Industrious soldiership.

SIWARD.

The time approaches
That will with due decision make us know
What we shall say we have and what we
owe.
Thoughts speculative their unsure hopes
relate,
But certain issue strokes must arbitrate:
Towards which advance the war.

[*Exeunt, marching.*

Scene V.

Dunsinane. Within the castle.
Enter MACBETH, SEYTON, *and* SOLDIERS,
with drum and colours.

MACBETH.

Hang out our banners on the outward walls;
The cry is still, 'They come:' our castle's strength
Will laugh a siege to scorn: here let them lie
Till famine and the ague eat them up:
Were they not forced with those that should be ours,
We might have met them dareful, beard to beard,
And beat them backward home.
                    [*A cry of women within.*
                    What is that noise?
SEYTON.

It is the cry of women, my good lord.
                        [*Exit.*
MACBETH.

I have almost forgot the taste of fears;
The time has been, my senses would have cool'd
To hear a night-shriek; and my fell of hair

149

Would at a dismal treatise rouse and stir
As life were in't: I have supp'd full with
horrors;
Direness, familiar to my slaughterous thoughts
Cannot once start me.

Enter SEYTON.

                              Wherefore was that cry?
SEYTON.
  The queen, my lord, is dead.
MACBETH.
  She should have died hereafter;
There would have been a time for such a
word. —
Tomorrow, and tomorrow, and tomorrow,
Creeps in this petty pace from day to day
To the last syllable of recorded time,
And all our yesterdays have lighted fools
The way to dusty death. Out, out, brief
candle!
Life's but a walking shadow, a poor player
That struts and frets his hour upon the
stage
And then is heard no more: it is a tale
Told by an idiot, full of sound and fury,
Signifying nothing.

Enter a MESSENGER.

Thou comest to use thy tongue; thy story
quickly.

MESSENGER.
  Gracious my lord,
  I should report that which I say I saw,
  But know not how to do it.
MACBETH.
                              Well, say, sir.
MESSENGER.
  As I did stand my watch upon the hill,
  I look'd toward Birnam, and anon, methought,
  The wood began to move.
MACBETH.
                              Liar and slave!
MESSENGER.
  Let me endure your wrath, if't be not so:
  Within this three mile may you see it coming;
  I say, a moving grove.
MACBETH.
                              If thou speak'st false,
  Upon the next tree shalt thou hang alive,
  Till famine cling thee: if thy speech be
  sooth,
  I care not if thou dost for me as much. —
  I pull in resolution, and begin
  To doubt the equivocation of the fiend
  That lies like truth: 'Fear not, till Birnam
  wood
  Do come to Dunsinane:' — and now a
  wood
  Comes toward Dunsinane. — Arm, arm, and
  out!
  If this which he avouches does appear,
  There is nor flying hence nor tarrying here.

I 'gin to be aweary of the sun,
And wish the estate o' the world were now
undone. —
Ring the alarum-bell! — Blow, wind! come,
wrack!
At least we'll die with harness on our back.
                                    [*Exeunt.*

Scene VI.

The same. A plain before the castle.
Drum and colours. Enter MALCOLM, SIWARD,
MACDUFF, *&c., and their* ARMY, *with boughs.*

MALCOLM.
Now near enough; your leafy screens throw
down.
And show like those you are. — You, worthy
uncle,
Shall, with my cousin, your right-noble son,
Lead our first battle: worthy Macduff and
we
Shall take upon 's what else remains to do,
According to our order.
SIWARD.

Fare you well. —
Do we but find the tyrant's power tonight,
Let us be beaten, if we cannot fight.
MACDUFF.
Make all our trumpets speak; give them all
breath,
Those clamorous harbingers of blood and
death.

[*Exeunt.*

153

Scene VII.

The same. Another part of the plain.
Alarums. Enter MACBETH.

MACBETH.

They have tied me to a stake; I cannot fly,
But, bear-like, I must fight the course.
— What's he
That was not born of woman? Such a one
Am I to fear, or none.

Enter YOUNG SIWARD.

YOUNG SIWARD.
What is thy name?

MACBETH.

     Thou'lt be afraid to hear it.

YOUNG SIWARD.
No; though thou call'st thyself a hotter name
Than any is in hell.

MACBETH.

     My name's Macbeth.

YOUNG SIWARD.
The devil himself could not pronounce a title
More hateful to mine ear.

MACBETH.

     No, nor more fearful.

YOUNG SIWARD.

Thou liest, abhorred tyrant; with my sword
I'll prove the lie thou speak'st.

[*They fight and* YOUNG SIWARD *is slain.*

MACBETH.

Thou wast born of woman
But swords I smile at, weapons laugh to
scorn,
Brandish'd by man that's of a woman born.

[*Exit.*

Alarums. Enter MACDUFF.

MACDUFF.

That way the noise is. — Tyrant, show thy
face!
If thou be'st slain and with no stroke of
mine,
My wife and children's ghosts will haunt
me still.
I cannot strike at wretched kerns, whose
arms
Are hired to bear their staves: either thou,
Macbeth,
Or else my sword with an unbatter'd edge
I sheathe again undeeded. There thou shouldst
be;
By this great clatter, one of greatest note
Seems bruited. — Let me find him, Fortune!
And more I beg not.

[*Exit. Alarums.*

Enter MALCOLM *and* SIWARD.

SIWARD.

This way, my lord; — the castle's gently render'd:
The tyrant's people on both sides do fight;
The noble thanes do bravely in the war;
The day almost itself professes yours,
And little is to do.

MALCOLM.

               We have met with foes
That strike beside us.

SIWARD.

Enter, sir, the castle.

               [*Exeunt. Alarums.*

Scene VIII.

The same. Another part of the plain.
Enter MACBETH.

MACBETH.
Why should I play the Roman fool, and die
On mine own sword? whiles I see lives, the gashes
Do better upon them.

Enter MACDUFF.

MACDUFF.
                   Turn, hell-hound, turn!
MACBETH.
Of all men else I have avoided thee:
But get thee back; my soul is too much charged
With blood of thine already.
MACDUFF.
I have no words, ——
My voice is in my sword; thou bloodier villain
Than terms can give thee out!
                  [*They fight. Alarum.*
MACBETH.
             Thou losest labour:

As easy mayst thou the intrenchant air
With thy keen sword impress as make me
bleed:
Let fall thy blade on vulnerable crests;
I bear a charmed life, which must not yield,
To one of woman born.

MACDUFF.

                     Despair thy charm;
And let the angel whom thou still hast
served
Tell thee, Macduff was from his mother's
womb
Untimely ripp'd.

MACBETH.

Accursed be that tongue that tells me so,
For it hath cow'd my better part of man!
And be these juggling fiends no more believed,
That palter with us in a double sense;
That keep the word of promise to our ear,
And break it to our hope. — I'll not fight
with thee.

MACDUFF.

Then yield thee, coward,
And live to be the show and gaze o' the
time:
We'll have thee, as our rarer monsters are,
Painted upon a pole, and underwrit,
'Here may you see the tyrant.'

MACBETH.

                     I will not yield,
To kiss the ground before young Malcolm's
feet,

And to be baited with the rabble's curse.
Though Birnam wood be come to Dunsinane,
And thou opposed, being of no woman
born,
Yet I will try the last: — before my body
I throw my warlike shield: Lay on, Macduff,
And damn'd be him that first cries, 'Hold,
enough!'

[*Exeunt, fighting.*

Enter fighting, and MACBETH *slain.*
Retreat. Flourish. Enter, with drum and colours,
MALCOLM, SIWARD, ROSS, THANES, *and* SOLDIERS.

MALCOLM.
I would the friends we miss were safe arrived.
SIWARD.
Some must go off: and yet, by these I
see,
So great a day as this is cheaply bought.
MALCOLM.
Macduff is missing, and your noble son.
ROSS.
Your son, my lord, has paid a soldier's
debt:
He only lived but till he was a man;
The which no sooner had his prowess
confirm'd
In the unshrinking station where he fought,
But like a man he died.
SIWARD.

Then he is dead?

ROSS.

Ay, and brought off the field: your cause of sorrow

Must not be measured by his worth, for then

It hath no end.

SIWARD.

Had he his hurts before?

ROSS.

Ay, on the front.

SIWARD.

Why then, God's soldier be he!

Had I as many sons as I have hairs,

I would not wish them to a fairer death:

And so, his knell is knoll'd.

MALCOLM.

He's worth more sorrow,

And that I'll spend for him.

SIWARD.

He's worth no more:

They say he parted well, and paid his score:

And so, God be with him! — Here comes newer comfort.

Enter MACDUFF, *with* MACBETH'S *head.*

MACDUFF.

Hail, king! for so thou art: behold, where stands

The usurper's cursed head: the time is free:

I see thee compass'd with thy kingdom's pearl,

That speak my salutation in their minds;
Whose voices I desire aloud with mine, —
Hail, King of Scotland!
ALL.

> Hail, King of Scotland!
> [*Flourish.*

MALCOLM.
We shall not spend a large expense of time
Before we reckon with your several loves,
And make us even with you. My thanes and
kinsmen,
Henceforth be earls, — the first that ever
Scotland
In such an honour named. What's more
to do,
Which would be planted newly with the
time, —
As calling home our exiled friends abroad
That fled the snares of watchful tyranny;
Producing forth the cruel ministers
Of this dead butcher and his fiend-like
queen, —
Who, as 'tis thought, by self and violent
hands
Took off her life; — this, and what needful
else
That calls upon us, by the grace of Grace,
We will perform in measure, time and place:
So, thanks to all at once and to each one,
Whom we invite to see us crown'd at Scone.
> [*Flourish. Exeunt.*

Glossary

ABATE: to shorten. To cast down. To blunt.
ABATEMENT: diminution.
ABIDE: to sojourn. to expiate (a corruption of 'Aby').
ABLE: to uphold.
ABRIDGEMENT: a short play.
ABROOK: to brook, abide.
ABSEY-BOOK: a primer.
ABSOLUTE: positive, certain. Complete.
ABUSE: to deceive. Deception.
ABY: to expiate a fault.
ABYSM: abyss.
ACCITE: to cite, summon.
ACCUSE: accusation.
ACHIEVE: to obtain.
ACKNOWN: 'to be acknown' is to acknowledge.
ACQUITTANCE: a receipt or discharge.
ACTION-TAKING: litigious.
ACTURE: action.
ADDITION: title, attribute.
ADDRESS: prepare oneself.
ADVANCE: to prefer, promote to honour.
ADVERTISEMENT: admonition.
ADVERTISING: attentive.
ADVICE: consideration, discretion.
ADVISE: to consider, reflect.

165

ADVISED: considerate.

ADVOCATION: pleading, advocacy.

AFEARED: afraid.

AFFECT: to love.

AFFEERED: assessed, confirmed.

AFFY: to affiance. To trust.

AFRONT: in front.

AGAZED: looking in amazement.

AGLET-BABY: the small figure engraved on a jewel.

AGNISE: to acknowledge, confess.

A-GOOD: a good deal, plenteously.

A-HOLD: a sea-term.

AIM: a guess.

ALDER-LIEFEST: most loved of all.

ALE: alehouse.

ALLOW: to approve.

ALLOWANCE: approval.

ALLYCHOLLY: melancholy.

AMES-ACE: two aces, the lowest throw of the dice.

AMORT: dead, dejected.

AN: if.

ANCHOR: an anchorite, hermit.

ANCIENT: an ensign-bearer.

ANGEL: a coin, bearing the image of an angel.

ANIGHT: by night.

ANSWER: retaliation.

ANTHROPOPHAGINIAN: a cannibal.

ANTICK: the fool in the old plays.

ANTRE: a cave.

APPARENT: heir-apparent.

APPEAL: accusation. Accuse.

APPEARED: made apparent.

APPLE-JOHN: a kind of apple.

APPOINTMENT: preparation.

APPREHENSION: opinion.

APPREHENSIVE: apt to apprehend or understand.

APPROBATION: probation.

APPROOF: approbation, proof.

APPROVE: to prove. To justify, make good.

APPROVER: one who proves or tries.

ARCH: chief.

ARGAL: ergo, therefore.

ARGENTINE: silver.

ARGIER: Algiers.

ARGOSY: a merchant ship, originally of Ragusa.

ARGUMENT: subject.

ARMIGERO: Esquire.

AROINT: get thee gone.

A-ROW: in a row.

ARTICULATE: to enter into articles of agreement.

ASK: to require.

ASPECT: regard, looks.

ASPERSION: sprinkling; hence blessing, generally
    accompanied by the sprinkling of holy water.

ASSAY: attempt, test, make proof of.

ASSINEGO: an ass.

ASSUBJUGATE: to subjugate.

ASSURANCE: deed of assurance.

ASSURED: betrothed.

ATOMY: an atom, a small person.

ATONE: to put people at one, to reconcile.

ATTACH: to seize, lay hold on.

ATTASKED: taken to task, reprehended.

ATTEND: to listen to.

ATTENT: attentive.

ATTORNEY: an agent.

ATTORNEY: to employ as an agent. To perform by an agent.

AUDACIOUS: spirited, daring.

AUGUR: augury.

AUTHENTIC: clothed with authority.

AVAUNT: be gone, a word of abhorrence.

AVE: hail.

AVE-MARY: salutation addressed to the Blessed Virgin Mary.

AVERRING: confirming.

AWFUL: worshipful.

AWKWARD: contrary.

BACCARE: keep back.

BACKWARD: the hinder part; the past.

BALKED: heaped, as on a ridge.

BALLOW: a cudgel.

BALM: the oil of consecration.

BAN: to curse.

BANK: to sail by the banks.

BARM: yeast.

BARN: a child.

BARNACLE: a shellfish, supposed to produce the sea-bird of the same name.

BASE: a game, sometimes called Prisoners' base.

BASES: an embroidered mantle worn by knights on horseback, reaching below the knees.

BASILISK: a kind of ordnance.

BASTA: (Italian), enough.

BASTARD: raisin wine.

BATE: to flutter, as a hawk. To abate.

BAT-FOWLING: catching birds with a clap-net by night.

BATLET: a small bat, used for beating clothes.

BATTLE: army.

BAVIN: like brushwood, blazing and instantly dying.

BAWCOCK: a fine fellow.

BAY: the space between the roof timbers.

BEADSMAN: one who says prayers for another.

BEARING-CLOTH: a christening robe.

BEAT: to flutter as a falcon, to meditate, consider earnestly.

BEAVER: the lower part of a helmet.

BEETLE: a mallet.

BEING: dwelling.

BE-METE: to measure.

BE-MOILED: daubed with dirt.

BENVENUTO: (Italian), welcome.

BERGOMASK: a rustic dance.

BESHREW: evil befall; a plague upon.

BESTRAUGHT: distraught, distracted.

BETEEM: to pour out. To allow.

BETID: happened.

BEZONIAN: a beggarly fellow.

BIDING: abiding-place.

BIGGEN: a night-cap.

BILBERRY: the whortleberry.

BILBO: a sword, from Bilbao in Spain.

BILBOES: fetters or stocks.

BILL: a bill-hook, a weapon.

BIN: been, are.

BIRD-BOLT: an arrow for shooting at birds.

BIRDING: hawking at partridges.

BISSON: blind.

BLANK: the white mark in the middle of a target.

BLENCH: to start aside, flinch.

BLENT: blended.

BLOOD-BOLTERED: smeared with blood.

BLOW: to inflate.

BOARD: to accost.

BOB: a blow, or hit; a gibe. To cheat.

BODGE: to botch, bungle.

BODIKIN: 'Od's Bodikin', God's little body.

BOITIER VERT: (French), green box.

BOLLEN: swollen.

BOLTED: sifted, refined.

BOLTER: a sieve.

BOLTING-HUTCH: a container for sifting meal.

BOMBARD: a barrel, a drunkard.

BOMBAST: padding.

BONA-ROBA: a harlot.

BOND: that to which one is bound.

BOOK: a paper of conditions.

BOOT: help, use.

BOOTS: bots, a kind of worm.

BORE: calibre of a gun; hence, metaph. size, weight, importance.

BOSKY: covered with underwood.

BOSOM: wish, heart's desire.

BOTS: worms which infest horses.

BOURN: a boundary. A brook.

BRACE: armour for the arm, state of defence.

BRACH: a hound bitch.

BRAID: deceitful.

BRAVE: handsome, well-dressed.

BRAVE: boast.

BRAVERY: finery. Boastfulness.

BRAWL: a kind of dance.

BREAST: voice.

BREATHE: to exercise.

BREECHING: liable to be whipped.

BREED-BATE: a fomenter of trouble or debate.

BREESE: the gadfly.

BRIBE-BUCK: a buck given away in presents.

BRING: to attend one on a journey.

BROCK: a badger.

BROKE: to act as a procurer.

BROKEN: having lost some teeth by age.

BROKEN MUSIC: the music of stringed instruments.

BROKER: an agent.

BROTHERHOOD: trading company.

BROWNIST: a sectary, a follower of Brown, the founder of the Independents.

BRUIT: noise, report, rumour.

BRUSH: rude assault.

BUCK: suds or lye for washing clothes in.

BUCK-BASKET: a soiled clothes basket.

BUCKING: washing.

BUCK-WASHING: washing in lye.

BUG: a bugbear, a spectre.

BULLY-ROOK: a bragging cheater.

BURGONET: a kind of helmet.

BURST: to break.

BUSKY: bushy.

BUTT-SHAFT: a light arrow for shooting at a target.

BUXOM: obedient.

BY'RLAKIN: by our little Lady: an oath.

CADDIS: worsted galloon, or trimming tape.

CADE: a cask or barrel.

CAGE: a prison.

CAIN-COLOURED: red (applied to hair).

CAITIFF: a captive, a slave; a mean fellow.

CALCULATE: prophesy.

CALIVER: a hand-gun.

CALLET: a trull.

CALLING: appellation.

CALM: qualm.

CAN: to know, be skilful in.

CANAKIN: a little can.

CANARY: a wine brought from the Canary Islands.

CANDLE-WASTERS: persons who sit up all night to drink.

CANKER: a caterpillar. The dog-rose.

CANSTICK: a candlestick.

CANTLE: a slice, corner.

CANTON: a canto.

CANVAS: to sift: hence, metaphorically, to prove.

CAPABLE: subject to. Intelligent. Capable of inheriting. Ample, capacious.

CAPITULATE: make a combined force.

CAPOCCHIA: a simpleton.

CAPRICIO: (Italian), caprice.

CAPRICIOUS: lascivious.

CAPTIOUS: capacious.

CARACK: a large ship of burden.

CARBONADO: meat scotched for broiling.

CARD: the diagram of points on a mariner's compass.

CAREIRE: the curvetting of a horse.

CARKANET: a necklace.

CARL: a churl, a husbandman.

CARLOT: a churl, a husbandman.

CASTILIAN: a native of Castile; used as a cant term.

CASTILIANO VULGO: a cant term, meaning, apparently, to use discreet language.

CATAIAN: a native of Cathay, Chinese.

CATLING: cat-gut.

CAUTEL: deceit.

CAUTELOUS: insidious.

CAVALERO: a cavalier, gentleman.

CAVIARE: the roe of sturgeon pickled; metaph. a delicacy not appreciated by the vulgar.

CEASE: decease.

CENSURE: judgment. To judge, criticise.

CEREMONY: a ceremonial rite or vestment.

CERTES: certainly.

CESS: rate, reckoning.

CHACE: a term at tennis.

CHAMBER: a species of great gun.

CHAMBERER: an effeminate man.

CHANSON: a song.

CHARACT: affected quality.

CHARACTER: handwriting. Write, engrave.

CHARACTERY: handwriting. That which is written.

CHARE: a turn of work, a chore.

CHARGE-HOUSE: a free-school.

CHARLES' WAIN: the Great Bear, the Plough.

CHARNECO: a species of sweet wine.

CHAUDRON: entrails.

CHEATER: for escheator, an officer who collected the fines to be paid into the Exchequer.

CHECK AT: in falconry, when a falcon foresakes her proper quarry for baser game.

CHEER: fortune, countenance.

CHERRY-PIT: a game played with cherrystones.

CHEVERIL: kid leather.

CHEWIT: a cough, a chatterer.

CHILDING: pregnant.

CH'ILL: vulgar for 'I will'.

CHIRURGEONLY: in a manner becoming a surgeon.

CHOPIN: a high shoe or clog.

CHRISTENDOM: the state of being a Christian.

CHRISTOM: clothed with a chrisom, the white garment put on newly-baptized children.

CHUCK: chicken, a term of endearment.

CHUFF: a coarse blunt clown.

CINQUE PACE: a kind of dance.

CIPHER: to decipher.

CIRCUMSTANCE: an argument.

CITAL: recital.

CITE: to incite.

CITTERN: a guitar.

CLACK-DISH: a beggar's dish.

CLAP I' THE CLOUT: to shoot an arrow into the bull's eye of the target.

CLAW: to flatter.

CLEPE: to call.

CLIFF: clef, the key in music.

CLING: to starve.

CLINQUANT: glittering.

CLIP: to embrace, enclose.

CLOUT: the mark in the middle of a target.

COAST: to advance, approach.

COBLOAF: a big loaf.

COCK: a cockboat.

COCK: a euphemism for God.

COCKLE: tares or darnel.

COCKNEY: a milksop.

COCK-SHUT-TIME: the twilight, when cocks and hens go to roost.

COG: to cheat, dissemble.

COGNIZANCE: badge, token.

COIGN: projecting corner stone.

COIL: tumult, turmoil.

COISTREL: a cowardly knave.

COLLECTION: drawing a conclusion.

COLLIED: blackened, clouded.

COLOUR: pretence.

COLOURABLE: specious, plausible.

COLT: to defraud, befool.

CO-MART: a joint bargain.

COMBINATE: betrothed.

COMMODITY: interest, profit.

COMMONTY: used ludicrously for comedy.

COMPACT: compacted, composed.

COMPETITOR: an associate, a partner.

COMPLEMENT: accomplishment.

COMPLEXION: humour.

COMPOSE: to agree.

COMPOSTION: composition, agreement.

COMPTIBLE: tractable.

CON: to learn by heart. To acknowledge.

CONCEIT: conception, opinion, fancy.

CONCUPY: concubine.

CONDITION: temper, quality.

CONDOLEMENT: grief.

CONFECT: to make up into sweetmeats.

CONFOUND: to consume, destroy.

CONJECT: conjecture.

CONSIGN: to sign a common bond, to confederate.

CONSORT: to accompany.

CONSTANCY: consistency, fidelity.

CONSTANT: settled, determined.

CONSTER: to construe.

CONTEMPTIBLE: contemptuous.

CONTINENT: that which contains.

CONTINUATE: uninterrupted.

CONTRACTION: the marriage contract.

CONTRARY: to oppose.

CONTRIVE: to spend (time).

CONTROL: to confute.

CONVENT: to convene, summon, to be convenient.

CONVERTITE: a convert.

CONVEY: to manage. To filch.

CONVINCE: to conquer, subdue.

CONVIVE: to feast together.

CONY-CATCH: to cheat, to dupe.

176

COOLING CARD: anything that dashes hopes.

COPATAIN HAT: a high-crowned hat.

COPE: to reward, to give in return.

COPPED: rising to a cop or head.

COPY: theme, example.

CORAGIO: (Italian) courage!

CORAM: an ignorant mistake for Quorum.

CORANTO: lively dance.

CORINTH: a cant term for a brothel.

CORINTHIAN: a wencher.

CORKY: dry like cork, withered.

CORNUTO: (Italian) a cuckold.

COROLLARY: surplus, additional.

CORPORAL: corporeal, bodily.

CORPORAL OF THE FIELD: an aide-de-camp.

CORRIVAL: rival.

COSTARD: the head.

COSTER-MONGER: peddling, mercenary.

COTE: a cottage.

COTE: to come alongside, overtake. To quote.

COT-QUEAN: an effeminate man, molly-coddle.

COUNT CONFECT: an affected nobleman.

COUNTENANCE: pretend; give support to.

COUNTERFEIT: portrait. A piece of base coin.

COUNTERPOINT: a counterpane.

COUNTERVAIL: to counterpoise, outweigh.

COUNTY: count, earl.

COUPLEMENT: union.

COURT HOLY-WATER: flattery.

COVENT: a convent.

COVER: to lay the table for dinner.

COWISH: cowardly.

COWL-STAFF: the staff for carrying a tub.

COX MY PASSION: an oath, for 'God's Passion'.

COY: to stroke, fondle. To show disdain.

COZEN: to cheat.

COZIER: a tailor or cobbler.

CRACK: to boast.

CRACK: a loud noise, clap. A forward boy.

CRACK-HEMP: a gallows-bird.

CRANK: a winding passage. To twist and turn.

CRANTS: garlands.

CRARE: a ship of burden.

CRAVEN: a dunghill cock, a coward.

CREATE: formed, compounded.

CREDENT: creditable. Credible. Credulous.

CRESCIVE: increasing.

CRESTLESS: not entitled to bear arms, lowborn.

CRISP: curled, winding.

CROSS: a coin stamped with a cross.

CROW-KEEPER: one who scares crows.

CROWNER: a coroner.

CROWNET: a coronet.

CRY: a pack of hounds or knaves.

CRY AIM: to encourage.

CUE: the last words of an actor's speech, the signal for the next actor to begin.

CUISSES: pieces of armour to cover the thighs.

CULLION: a base fellow.

CUNNING: skill, skilful.

CURB: to bend, truckle.

CURRENTS: occurrences.

CURST: shrewish, sharp tempered.

CURTAIL: a cur.

CURTAL: a docked horse.

CURTAL-AXE: a cutlass.

CUSTALORUM: a ludicrous mistake for Custos Rotulorum, a chief justice.

CUSTARD-COFFIN: the crust of a custard-pudding.

CUSTOMER: a common woman.

CUT: a cheat. 'To draw cuts' is to draw lots.

CYPRESS: a kind of crape.

DAFF: to befool. To put off.

DANGER: reach, control, power.

DANSKER: a Dane.

DARRAIGN: to set in array.

DAUB: to disguise.

DAUBERY: imposition, falsehood.

DEARN: hidden, solitary.

DEBOSHED: debauched, drunken.

DECK: to bedew, to adorn.

DECLINE: to enumerate.

DEEM: doom, judgment.

DEFEAT: to undo, destroy. Destruction.

DEFEATURE: disfigurement.

DEFENCE: art of fencing.

DEFEND: to forbid.

DEFY: renounce.

DEGREE: relative position or rank.

DEMERIT: merit, desert.

DENAY: denial.

DENIER: the 12th part of a French sou coin.

DENY: to refuse.

DEPEND: to be in service.

DEROGATE: degraded, debased.

DESCANT: comment on a given theme.

DETECT: to charge, blame.

DETERMINE: to conclude.

DICH: may it do.

DIFFUSED: confused.

DIGRESSION: transgression.

DIG-YOU-GOOD-DEN: give you good evening.

DILDO: the chorus or burden of a song.

DINT: stroke, impression.

DIRECTION: judgment, skill.

DISABLE: to disparage.

DISAPPOINTED: unprepared.

DISCASE: to undress.

DISCONTENT: a malcontent.

DISCOURSE: power of reasoning.

DISLIMN: to disfigure, transform, efface.

DISME: a tenth or tithe.

DISPARK: to destroy a park.

DISPONGE: to squeeze out as from a sponge.

DISPOSE: disposal, disposition. To arrange.

DISPOSITION: arrangement; behaviour.

DISPUTABLE: disputatious.

DISSEMBLY: used ridiculously for assembly.

DISTASTE: to offend the taste, disgust.

DISTEMPERED: discontented, disturbed.

DISTRACTION: a detached troop or company of soldiers.

DIVISION: a phrase or passage in a melody.

DOFF: to take off, remove. To put off with an excuse.

DOIT: a small Dutch coin, a trifle.

DOLE: portion dealt. Grief, lamentation.

DOTANT: one who dotes, a dotard.

DOUT: to quench.

DOWLAS: a kind of coarse sacking.

DOWLE: feather.

DOWN-GYVED: hanging down like gyves or fetters.

DRAB: a harlot.

DRAUGHT: a privy.

DRAWN: having his sword drawn.

DRIBBLING: falling wide of the mark.

DROLLERY: a puppet-show.

DRUMBLE: to dawdle.

DUC-DAME: duc-ad-me, bring him to me.

DUDGEON: hilt of a dagger.

DULL: soothing.

DUMP: sad tune.

DUP: lift up, undo.

EAGER: harsh, cutting, sour.

EANLING: a yeanling, a lamb.

EAR: to plough.

ECHE: to eke out.

ECSTACY: madness.

EFT: ready, convenient.

EISEL: vinegar.

ELD: old age.

EMBOSSED: swollen; foaming from exertion (of a hound).

EMBOWELLED: disembowelled.

EMBRASURE: embrace.

EMPERY: empire.

EMULATION: jealousy.

EMULOUS: jealous, ambitious.

ENCAVE: to place in a cave, to hide.

ENFEOFF: to hand over, surrender.

ENGINE: a machine of war.

ENGLUT: to swallow speedily.

ENGROSS: to make gross or fat.

ENGROSSMENT: immoderate acquisition.

ENKINDLE: to make keen.

ENMEW: to shut up, coop up.

ENSCONCE: to cover as with a fort; to take shelter.

ENSEAMED: fat, greasy.

ENSHIELD: guard, protect.

ENTERTAIN: take into service.

ENTERTAINMENT: treatment; reception.

ENTREATMENT: entreating.

EPHESIAN: a toper, a cant term.

EQUIPAGE: attendance, retinue.

EREWHILE: a short time since.

ESCOT: to pay a man's reckoning, to maintain.

ESPERANCE: hope, used as a war-cry.

ESPIAL: a scout or spy.

ESTIMATION: conjecture.

ESTRIDGE: ostrich.

EXCREMENT: outgrowths from the body like hair or nails.

EXECUTOR: an executioner.

EXEMPT: excluded, separated.

EXERCISE: a religious service.

EXHALE: to draw the sword.

EXHIBITION: allowance, pension.

182

EXIGENT: death, ending; emergency.

EXION: ridiculously used for 'action'.

EXPEDIENCE: purpose requiring haste.

EXPEDIENT: expeditious, swift.

EXPIATE: completed, fully arrived.

EXPOSTULATE: to expound, discuss.

EXPOSTURE: exposure.

EXPRESS: well made.

EXPULSE: to expel.

EXSUFFLICATE: contemptible, puffed out.

EXTEND: to seize, to magnify.

EXTERN: outward.

EXTIRP: to extirpate.

EXTRAUGHT: extracted, descended.

EXTRAVAGANT: foreign, wandering.

EYAS: a nestling hawk.

EYAS-MUSKET: a young sparrow-hawk, a sprightly boy.

EYE: a shade of colour, as in shot silk.

EYNE: eyes.

FACINOROUS: wicked.

FACT: guilt, crime.

FACTIOUS: instant, importunate.

FACULTY: essential virtue or power.

FADGE: to suit, turn out.

FADING: a kind of ending to a song.

FAIN: glad, gladly.

FAIR: beauty.

FAITOR: imposter, cheat.

FALLOW: fawn-coloured.

FALSING: deceptive.

FAMILIAR: a familiar spirit.

FANCY-FREE: untouched by love.

FANG: to seize.

FANTASTIC: a fantastical person.

FAP: drunk.

FARCED: stuffed out.

FARDEL: a burden.

FARTUOUS: used ridiculously for 'virtuous'.

FAT: hot; vat.

FAVOUR: countenance. Complexion. Quality.

FEAR: to frighten.

FEAT: dexterous, neat, becoming.

FEAT: to mirror, reflect.

FEATLY: nimbly, daintily.

FEATURE: beauty.

FEDERARY: confederate, accomplice.

FEEDER: agent, servant.

FEE-GRIEF: a private grief.

FEERE: a companion, spouse.

FEHEMENTLY: used ridiculously for 'vehemently'.

FELL: the hide.

FENCE: art or skill in defence.

FEODARY: one who holds an estate by suit or service to a superior lord; a dependant.

FESTINATELY: quickly.

FET: fetched.

FICO: a fig.

FIG: to insult.

FIGHTS: screens round a ship to conceal the men from the enemy.

FILE: to defile, pollute.

FILL-HORSE: shaft-horse.

184

FILLS: the shafts.

FINE: end.

FINELESS: endless.

FIRAGO: ridiculously used for 'Virago'.

FIRE-DRAKE: meteor;(slang) man with red nose.

FIRE-NEW: brand-new.

FIRK: to chastise.

FIT: a canto or division of a song. A trick or habit. A spasm.

FITCHEW: a polecat.

FIVES: a disease incident to horses.

FLAP-DRAGON: raisins in burning brandy.

FLAP-JACK: a pan-cake.

FLATNESS: depth.

FLAW: a gust of wind, or sudden emotion, fragment.

FLAW: to make a flaw in, to break.

FLECKED: spotted, streaked.

FLEET: to float. To pass away, to pass the time.

FLEETING: inconstant.

FLESHMENT: excitement arising from success.

FLEWED: with hanging chops, like hounds.

FLIGHT: archery contest.

FLIRT-GILL: a light woman.

FLOTE: wave, sea.

FLOURISH: ornament.

FLUSH: fresh, full of vigour, in full bloom.

FOIL: defeat, disadvantage.

FOIN: to fence, fight.

FOISON: plenty, abundance.

FOND: foolish, foolishly affectionate.

FOOT-CLOTH: a saddle-cloth hanging down to the ground.

FORBID: accursed, outlawed.

FORBODE: forbidden.

FORCE: to stuff, to cram.

FORDO: to kill, destroy. To weary.

FOREIGN: obliged to live abroad.

FOREPAST: former.

FORESLOW: to delay.

FORFEND: to forbid.

FORGETIVE: inventive.

FORKED: horned. Two-legged.

FORMAL: regular, normal.

FORSPEAK: to speak against.

FORSPENT: exhausted, weary.

FORTHRIGHT: a straight path.

FORWEARY: to weary, exhaust.

FOSSET-SELLER: seller of taps (faucets) for barrels.

FOX: a sword; a cant word.

FOX-SHIP: the cunning of the fox.

FRAMPOLD: peevish, disagreeable.

FRANK: the feeding place of swine, sty.

FRANKED: confined.

FRANKLIN: a freeholder, a small squire.

FRAUGHT: freight, the cargo of a ship.

FRAUGHTING: freight, the cargo of a ship.

FRESH: a spring of fresh water.

FRET: the stop of a musical instrument.

FRET: to wear away. To variegate, adorn.

FRIEND: to befriend.

FRIPPERY: an old-clothes shop.

FRONT: to affront, oppose.

FRONTIER: fortress.

FRONTLET: that which is worn on the forehead.

FRUSH: to break or bruise.

FRUSTRATE: frustrated.

FUB OFF: to put off.

FULFIL: to fill full.

FULLAM: a loaded die.

FULSOME: lustful, offensive.

GABERDINE: a loose outer coat, or smock frock.

GAD: a pointed instrument. Upon the gad, with impetuous haste, on the spur of the moment.

GAIN-GIVING: misgiving.

GALLIARD: a kind of dance.

GALLIASSE: a kind of ship.

GALLIMAUFRY: a ridiculous medley.

GALLOW: to scare.

GALLOWGLASS: the irregular infantry of Ireland, and the Highlands of Scotland.

GAMESTER: a frolicsome person. A loose woman.

GARBOIL: disorder, uproar.

GARNER: to lay by, as corn in a barn.

GAST: frightened.

GAUDY: festive.

GAZE: an object of wonder.

GEAR: matter of business of any kind.

GECK: a fool, butt.

GENERAL: the generality, the people.

GENEROSITY: noble birth.

GENEROUS: noble.

GENTILITY: good manners.

GENTLE: noble, well-born. To ennoble.

GENTRY: gentlemanly behaviour.

GERMAN: akin. Appropriate.

GERMEN: seed, embryo.

GEST: period; deed.

GIB: a he-cat.

GIFTS: talents, endowment.

GIGLOT: a wanton girl.

GILDER: a coin of the value of 1s. 6d. or 2s.

GIMMAL: double, jointed.

GIMMOR: contrivance.

GING: gang.

GLEEK: to scoff.

GLOSE: to comment; to intercept.

GLUT: to swallow.

GNARL: to snarl.

GOOD-DEED: indeed.

GOOD-DEN: good-evening.

GOOD-YEAR!: an oath (What the good year!)

GORBELLIED: corpulent.

GOURD: false dice.

GOUT: a drop.

GOVERNMENT: discretion, control.

GRACIOUS: abounding in grace.

GRAINED: engrained, dyed.

GRAMERCY: much thanks.

GRANGE: the farmstead attached to a monastery, a solitary farm-house.

GRATILLITY: a nonce-word: 'gratuity'.

GRATULATE: to congratulate.

GRAVE: to bury.

GREASILY: grossly.

GREEK: a bawd, buffoon.

GREENLY: foolishly.

GREET: to weep.

GRIZE: a step.

GROUNDLING: one who frequents the pit of a theatre.

GUARD: decoration, ornament.

GUARDAGE: guardianship.

GUINEA-HEN: a courtesan.

GULES: red, a term in heraldry.

GUN-STONE: a cannon ball.

GUST: taste, relish.

GYVE: to fetter.

HACK: to become common.

HAGGARD: a wild or unreclaimed hawk.

HAG-SEED: seed or offspring of a hag.

HAIR: grain, nature.

HALIDOM: holiness, used as an oath.

HALLOWMAS: All Hallows' Day.

HAP: chance, fortune.

HAPPILY: accidentally.

HANDSAW: perhaps a corruption of heronshaw; a heron.

HARDIMENT: defiance, brave deeds.

HARRY: to annoy, harass.

HAUGHT: haughty.

HAUNT: company.

HAUTBOYS: oboes.

HAVING: property, fortune.

HAVIOUR: behavior.

HAY: a term in fencing; a dance.

HEADY: violent, headlong.

HEBENON: henbane.

HEFT: a heaving.

HELM: to steer, manage.

HENCE: henceforward.

HENCHMAN: a page or attendant.

HENT: grasp, occasion for seizing.

HERMIT: a beadsman.

HEST: command, behest.

HIGHT: called.

HILD: pp. held.

HILDING: a paltry fellow.

HIREN: a prostitute, with a pun on the word 'iron'.

HOISE: to hoist, heave up on high.

HOIST: hoisted.

HOLP: helped.

HOME: to the utmost, fully.

HONEST: chaste, modest.

HONESTY: chastity.

HONEY-STALKS: red clover.

HOODMAN-BLIND: blindman's-buff.

HORN-MAD: furious, enraged.

HOROLOGE: a clock.

HOT-HOUSE: a brothel.

HOX: to hamstring.

HUGGER-MUGGER: secrecy.

HULL: to drift on the sea like a wrecked ship.

HUMOROUS: humid; full of humours.

HUNT-COUNTER: to follow the scent the wrong way.

HUNTS-UP: a hunting cry for daybreak.

HURLY: noise, confusion.
HURTLE: to clash noisily.
HUSBANDRY: frugality. Management.
HUSWIFE: a jilt.

ICE-BROOK: an icy-cold brook to temper steel.
I'FECKS: in faith, a euphemism.
IGNOMY: ignominy.
IMAGE: representation.
IMBARE: to bare, lay open.
IMMEDIACY: close connexion.
IMMOMENT: unimportant.
IMP: to graft, to splice a falcon's broken feathers.
IMP: a scion, a child.
IMPAWN: to stake, to risk.
IMPEACH: to bring into question. Impeachment.
IMPEACHMENT: cause of censure, hindrance.
IMPERCEIVERANT: undiscerning.
IMPETICOS: to pocket.
IMPORTANCE: importunity.
IMPORTANT: importunate.
IMPOSITION: command.
IMPRESE: a device with a motto.
IMPRESS: to compel to serve.
INCAPABLE: unconscious, unaware.
INCARNARDINE: to dye red.
INCENSED: incited, enraged.
INCH-MEAL: inch by inch.
INCLINING: inclination; compliant.
INCLIP: to embrace.
INCLUDE: conclude.
INCONY: fine, delicate.

INCORRECT: ill-regulated.

IND: India.

INDENT: to compound or bargain.

INDEX: a preface, contents.

INDIFFERENT: ordinary.

INDIGEST: shapeless mass.

INDITE: to invite. To convict.

INDUCTION: introduction, beginning.

INHABITABLE: uninhabitable.

INHERIT: to possess.

INHOOPED: penned up in hoops.

INKHORN-MATE: a contemptuous term for an ecclesiastic, or man of learning.

INKLE: a narrow fillet or tape.

INLAND: civilized, well-educated.

INLY: inwardly.

INSANE: that which causes insanity.

INSTANCE: example. Information. Reason, proof.

INTEND: to pretend.

INTENDMENT: intention.

INTENTIVELY: attentively.

INTERESSED: allied, interested.

INTRINSE: intricate.

INTRINSICATE: intricate.

INVENTION: imagination.

INWARD: an intimate friend; intimate.

INWARDNESS: intimacy.

IRREGULOUS: lawless, licentious.

JACK: a mean fellow.

JACK-A-LENT: a puppet thrown at in Lent.

JACK GUARDANT: a jack in office.

JADE: to whip, to treat with contempt.

JAR: the ticking of a clock.

JAUNCE: to cause a horse to prance; to trudge about.

JESS: a strap attached to the talons of a hawk.

JEST: to tilt in a tournament, to joust.

JET: to strut.

JOURNAL: daily.

JOVIAL: appertaining to Jove.

JUDICIOUS: critical.

JUMP: hazard.

JUMP: exactly, nicely.

JUT: to encroach.

JUTTY: jut out beyond; projection.

JUVENAL: youth, young man.

KAM: crooked, twisted.

KECKSY: hemlock-like weed.

KEECH: a lump of tallow.

KEEL: to skim, to cool.

KERN: the rude foot soldiers of the Irish.

KIBE: a chilblain.

KICKSHAWS: fancy trifles of food; frivolities.

KICKSY WICKSY: a wife, used in disdain.

KILN-HOLE: oven.

KINDLE: to bring forth young; used only of beasts.

KINDLESS: unnatural.

KINDLY: natural, generous.

KIRTLE: a gown.

KNAP: to snap, knock.

KNAVE: a boy. A serving-man.

KNOT: flower bed.

LABRAS: lips.

LACED-MUTTON: a courtezan.

LAG: the lowest of the people.

LAG: late, behindhand.

LAKIN: ladykin, little lady, 'By'r lakin': an oath.

LAND-DAMN: a term of abuse.

LAPSED: taken, apprehended.

LARGE: licentious, free.

LARGESS: a present.

LASS-LORN: deserted by a mistress.

LATCH: to smear. To catch.

LATED: belated.

LATTEN: made of brass.

LAUND: lawn, clearing in a forest.

LAVOLTA: a dance.

LAY: wager.

LEAGUE: besieging army.

LEASING: lying.

LEATHER-COATS: russet apples.

LEECH: a physician.

LEER: countenance, complexion.

LEET: a manor court.

LEGE: to allege.

LEGERITY: lightness.

LEIGER: an ambassador resident abroad.

LEMAN: a lover or mistress.

LENTEN: meagre; appropriate to Lent.

L'ENVOY: the final stanza of a poem.

LET: hindrance; to hinder.

LETHE: death. A river in Hades.

LEVEL: to aim.

LEWD: ignorant, base.

LEWDSTER: a lewd person.

LIBBARD: a leopard.

LIBERAL: licentious.

LIBERTY: libertinism.

LIEF: dear. Willingly.

LIFTER: a thief.

LIGHT O' LOVE: a tune so called.

LIGHTLY: easily, generally.

LIKE: to liken, compare.

LIKE: likely.

LIKING: condition.

LIMBECK: an alembick, a still.

LIMBO: the abode of the just who died before Christ's coming; slang for prison.

LIME: to entangle as with bird-lime. To mix lime with beer or other liquor.

LIMN: to draw or paint.

LINE: support.

LINSTOCK: a staff with a match at the end used by gunners in firing cannon.

LIST: a strip of cloth: an enclosure for tilting.

LITHER: lazy.

LITTLE: miniature.

LIVELIHOOD: appearance of life.

LIVERY: legal proceedings to recover an inheritance.

LOB: a lout.

LOCKRAM: a sort of coarse linen.

LODE-STAR: the leading-star, pole-star.

LOGGATS: the game called nine-pins.

LOOF: to luff, bring a vessel up to the wind.

LOON: a low contemptible fellow.

LOTTERY: a prize.

LOUT: to treat one as a lout, with contempt.

LOZEL: a rascal.

LUBBER: a lout, a clumsy fellow.

LUCE: the pike or jack, a fresh-water fish.

LUNES: fits of lunacy.

LURCH: to outdo, to deprive of all chance.

LURE: a dummy bird to attract a hawk.

LUXURIOUS: lascivious.

LUXURY: lust.

LYM: a bloodhound.

MAGNIFICO: a Venetian nobleman.

MAGGOT-PIE: a magpie.

MAIL: cover as with a coat of mail.

MAIN-COURSE: the mainsail.

MAKE: to do up, bar.

MALKIN: a servant wench.

MALLECHO: mischief.

MAMMERING: hesitating.

MAMMET: a doll, a puppet.

MAMMOCK: tear to pieces.

MAN: to tame a hawk.

MANAGE: management, control of a horse.

MANDRAGORA or MANDRAKE: a plant of soporiferous quality, supposed to resemble a man.

MANKIND: having a masculine nature.

MARCHES: frontiers, borders.

MARCHPANE: a sweetmeat like marzipan.

MARGENT: margin.

MARRY: an exclamation of surprise, indignation, etc.

MARTLEMAS: Martinmas, 11th November, a word applied derisively to an old man.

MATCH: a compact, agreement.

MATE: to confound, dismay.

MEACOCK: tame, cowardly.

MEALED: mingled, stained.

MEAN: instrument used to promote an end; opportunity.

MEAN: the tenor part in a harmony.

MEASURE: traverse. A stately dance.

MEAZEL: a leper.

MEDAL: a portrait in a locket.

MEDICINE: a physician.

MEED: reward, hire. Merit.

MEINY: retinue.

MELL: to mix, to meddle.

MEMORISE: to cause to be remembered.

MEPHISTOPHILUS: the name of a familiar spirit.

MERCATANTE: (Italian), a foreign trader.

MESS: a company of four.

METAPHYSICAL: supernatural.

METE-YARD: measuring-wand.

MEW UP: to confine.

MICHER: a truant.

MILL-SIXPENCE: a milled sixpence.

MINCING: affected.

MISCREATE: illegitimate, deformed.

MISERY: avarice.

MISPRISE: to despise. To mistake.

MISPRISION: mistaking, scorning.

MISSIVE: messenger.

MISTEMPERED: tempered for an evil purpose.

MISTHINK: to think ill of.

MISTRESS: the jack in bowling.

MOBLED: muffled, veiled.

MODERN: commonplace.

MODULE: a model, image.

MOIETY: a portion.

MOME: a stupid person.

MONTHS-MIND: a monthly commemoration of the dead, a strong desire.

MOON-CALF: a nick-name applied to Caliban.

MOONISH: inconstant.

MOP: grimace.

MORISCO: a morris-dancer.

MORRIS-PIKE: Moorish-pike.

MORT: death, applied to animals of the chase.

MORTIFIED: ascetic.

MOSE: applied to disease in a horse.

MOTION: a puppet-show.

MOTLEY: the many-coloured coat of a fool; one who plays the fool.

MOTLEY-MINDED: foolish.

MOUSE-HUNT: a weasel. A woman chaser.

MOW: to make grimaces.

MOY: the French 'Moi', misinterpreted by Pistol as a coin.

MUCH: significant of contempt.

MUCH: used ironically.

MURE: a wall.

MUSS: a scramble, a children's game.

MUTINE: to mutiny; a mutineer.

NAPKIN: a handkerchief.
NAYWARD: towards denial, or unbelief.
NAYWORD: a catch-word, by-word.
NEB: beak, mouth.
NEELD: a needle.
NEIF: hand.
NEPHEW: a grandson, kinsman.
NETHER-STOCKS: stockings, the stocks.
NICK: score or reckoning.
NICK: to brand with folly.
NIGHTED: black as night.
NIGHT-RULE: nightly revel.
NINE MEN'S MORRIS: a game in which each side has nine pieces, 'men'; the area in which it is played.
NINNY: a fool, a simpleton.
NOBLE: a coin, worth 6s. 8d.
NODDY: a dolt, simpleton.
NONCE: for the nonce, for the occasion.
NOOK-SHOTTEN: indented with bays and creeks.
NOURISH: nurse.
NOVUM: a game at dice.
NUTHOOK: a hook for pulling down nuts, a beadle.

O: a circle, the globe.
OAR: to row as with oars.
OBSEQUIOUS: a dutiful observance of funeral.
OBSTACLE: obstinate.
OCCUPATION: working men.

OCCURENT: an incident.

OD'S: interj. euphemism for God's.

OD'S BODY: God's body.

OD'S PITTIKINS: God's pity.

OEILLIAD: an amorous glance.

O'ERPARTED: having too important a part to act.

OFFICE: function, service, office-holder.

OLD: slang; great, fine.

ONEYER: a banker. A doubtful word.

OPEN: to give tongue as a hound.

OPERANT: active.

OPPOSITE: adversary.

OPPOSITION: combat.

OR: before.

ORDINANCE: rank, order. That which is ordained.

ORGULOUS: proud.

ORT: leaving, refuse, fragment.

OSTENT: show, appearance.

OSTENTATION: show, appearance.

OUNCE: a beast of prey, a lynx.

OUPHE: a fairy, elf.

OUSEL-COCK: the blackbird.

OUT: in error, at variance.

OUT-LOOK: to face down, to outstare.

OUTWARD: outside, external appearance.

OWE: to own.

PACK: to plot, be in league.

PADDOCK: a toad.

PALABRAS: words, a cant term, from the Spanish.

PALE: an inclosure; to enclose.

PALL: to wrap as with a pall. To fail, be ruined.

PALMER: one who bears a palm-branch, in token of having made a pilgrimage to the Holy Land.

PALMY: flourishing.

PARCELLED: belonging to individuals.

PARD: the leopard.

PARITOR: an apparitor, summoner to a bishop's court.

PARLE: talk, parley.

PARLOUS: perilous. keen, shrewd.

PARTED: endowed, gifted.

PARTISAN: a pike.

PASH: the head.

PASH: to strike violently, to bruise, crush.

PASSANT: (of heraldic figures), walking.

PASSING: surpassingly, exceedingly.

PASSION: pain, compassion, grief.

PASSY-MEASURE: a stately dance, a pavane.

PASTRY: the room where pastry was made.

PATCH: a mean fellow, a clown.

PATCHERY: trickery.

PATH: to walk.

PATIENT: to make patient, to compose.

PATINE: the metal dish on which the bread is placed in the administration of the Eucharist.

PAUCA VERBA: few words.

PAUCAS: few, a cant word.

PAVIN: a dance, a pavane.

PAX: a small image of Christ.

PEAT: a term of endearment for a child.

PEDASCULE: a pedant, schoolmaster.

PEIZE: to balance, weigh down.

PELTING: paltry.

PERDU: lost. A sentry in a perilous post.

PERDURABLE: everlasting.

PERDY: a euphemism for Par Dieu.

PERFECT: certain, fully prepared.

PERIAPTS: charms worn round the neck.

PERJURE: a perjured person.

PERSPECTIVE: a telescope, or some sort of optical device.

PEW-FELLOW: a comrade.

PHEEZE: beat, chastise, settle.

PIA-MATER: the brain.

PICK: to pitch, throw.

PICKERS: (and stealers), the fingers, hands.

PICKT-HATCH: a place noted for brothels.

PIELED: shaven.

PILCHER: a scabbard. A pilchard.

PILL: to pillage.

PIN: a malady of the eye. The centre of a target.

PINFOLD: a pound, a place to confine lost cattle.

PIONED: meaning doubtful; perhaps trenched.

PLACKET: a petticoat-front. A woman.

PLAIN SONG: a simple air, the simple truth.

PLANCHED: made of boards.

PLANTATION: colonizing, planting a colony.

PLAUSIVE: plausible, acceptable.

PLEACHED: interwoven, folded.

POINT: a lace to hold up breeches.
POINT-DEVICE: derived from the French, faultless.
POISE: balance, weight, importance.
POLLED: shorn.
POMANDER: a perfumed ball.
POMEWATER: a kind of apple.
POOR-JOHN: salted fish.
POPINJAY: a parrot, a fop.
PORT: pomp, state, bearing. A gate.
PORTABLE: bearable.
PORTANCE: conduct, behavior.
POSSESS: to inform.
POTCH: to push violently, stab.
POTENT: a potentate.
POUNCET-BOX: a box for holding perfumes.
PRACTISE: wicked stratagem.
PRACTISANT: a confederate, conspirator.
PRANK: to dress up.
PRECEPT: a justice's summons, a warrant.
PREGNANT: fertile of invention. Ready. Obvious.
PRENOMINATE: to name beforehand, to prophesy.
PRE-ORDINANCE: old-established law.
PRESENCE: the presence-chamber. High bearing.
PREST: ready.
PRETENCE: design, plan.
PRETEND: to portend. To intend.
PREVENT: to anticipate.
PRICK: the mark denoting the hour on a dial.
PRICK: to incite. To mark off on a list.
PRICK-SONG: music sung in parts by note.
PRICKET: a stag of two years.
PRIG: thief.

PRIME: rank, lecherous.

PRIMERO: a game at cards.

PRINCIPALITY: one of the orders of angels.

PRINCOX: a coxcomb, forward fellow.

PRIZER: a prize-fighter.

PROCURE: to bring.

PROFACE: interj. may it do you good.

PROGRESS: a royal ceremonial journey.

PROJECT: to shape or contrive.

PROMPTURE: suggestion.

PRONE: ready, willing.

PROOF: strength of manhood.

PROPAGATE: to advance, to forward.

PROPAGATION: augmentation.

PROPER-FALSE: handsome deceiver.

PROPERTIED: endowed with the properties of.
  Treated as a property.

PROPOSE: To converse. To purpose.

PROROGUE: to defer.

PROVAND: provender.

PUCELLE: a virgin, the maid Joan of Arc.

PUDENCY: modesty.

PUGGING: thieving.

PUN: to pound.

PURCHASE: acquire, gain.

PUTTER-ON: an instigator.

PUTTER-OUT: one who lends money at interest.

PUTTOCK: a kite.

QUAIL: be afraid: to cause to quail. A loose
  woman.

QUAINT: curiously beautiful. Clever.

204

QUALIFY: to moderate.

QUALITY: Rank or condition. Natural gifts, skill.

QUARRY: game, a heap of game.

QUARTER: area assigned to a body of troops. Watch, guard.

QUAT: a pimple; used in contempt of a person.

QUEASY: squeamish, unsettled, ticklish.

QUELL: murder, slaughter.

QUENCH: to grow cool.

QUERN: a hand-mill.

QUEST: search, inquest, jury.

QUESTRIST: one who goes in search of another.

QUICK: living, pregnant, enlivening.

QUICKEN: to come to life.

QUIDDITY: subtlety, argument.

QUILLET: legal quibble.

QUINTAIN: a post for tilting at.

QUIP: sharp jest, a taunt.

QUIT: to requite, release, remit, pay back.

QUITTANCE: requital.

QUIVER: active, nimble.

QUOTE: to note, set down.

RABATO: a ruff, a collar.

RABBIT-SUCKER: a weasel, a baby rabbit.

RACE: breed; inherited nature, origin.

RACK: wreck, stretch, cause pain, misrepresent.

RACK: drifting cloud.

RAPTURE: a fit. Seizure, force of movement.

RASCAL: a lean deer.

RASH: quick, violent. To thrust in.

RATE: opinion, judgment, estimation.

RATE: to assign, to value. To scold.

RATOLORUM: corruption of Custos Rotulorum (Keeper of the Rolls).

RAUGHT: past tense of to reach.

RAVIN: ravenous. Devour.

RAWNESS: unprovided state, unprotected.

RAYED: arrayed, served, dirtied.

RAZED: slashed, cut ornamentally.

REBATE: to deprive of keenness.

REBECK: a three-stringed fiddle.

RECHEAT: to call back the hounds.

RECORD: to sing.

RECORDER: a flute.

RECURE: to cure, recover.

RED-LATTICE: suitable to an ale-house.

REDUCE: to bring back.

REECHY: smoky, dirty.

REFELL: to refute.

REFER: hand over, transfer.

REGIMENT: government.

REGREET: to salute, greet.

REGUERDON: requital, reward.

REMEMBER: to remind.

REMORSE: pity.

REMORSEFUL: full of pity, compassionate.

REMOTION: removal, remoteness.

REMOVED: remote, secluded.

RENDER: account, admission. To declare.

RENEGE: to renounce, to deny.

REPAIR: comfort. Resort, return.

REPEAL: to reverse the sentence of exile.

REPROOF: confutation.
REPUGN: to resist.
REQUIEM: mass for the dead.
RESOLVE: to satisfy. To dissolve.
RESPECT: consideration, comparison, esteem.
RESPECTIVE: respectful, thoughtful.
RETIRE: retreat, withdraw.
REVERB: to echo, reverberate.
REVOLT: a rebel.
RIB: to enclose as within ribs.
RIGGISH: wanton.
RIGOL: a circle.
RIPE: ready, mature.
RIVAGE: the shore.
RIVAL: a partner.
RIVALITY: equal rank.
RIVE: to fire, to split.
ROAD: a prostitute.
ROISTING: roistering, rousing.
ROMAGE: unusual stir, turmoil.
RONYON: a term of contempt used to a woman.
ROOD: the crucifix.
ROOK: a cheat.
ROPERY: roguery.
ROPE-TRICKS: trickery, roguery.
ROUND: to be with child.
ROUND: unceremonious.
ROUNDEL: a dance or song.
ROUNDURE: an enclosure; roundness.
ROUSE: carousal.
ROYNISH: mangy, scurvy.
RUBIOUS: ruddy, ruby-red.

RUDDOCK: the redbreast.
RUSH: a ring made of rushes.

SACRING-BELL: the little bell rung at mass to give notice that the elements are consecrated.
SAD: serious.
SAFE: sane, sound, secure.
SALT: lascivious, biting, tearful.
SANDED: sand coloured.
SANS: without.
SAUCY: lascivious.
SAW: a moral saying, a proverb.
SAY: assay, taste. Silken.
SCAFFOLDAGE: the gallery of a theatre.
SCALD: scurvy, scabby.
SCALE: to weigh in scales.
SCALL: a scab, a word of reproach.
SCAMBLE: to scramble.
SCAMEL: possibly sea-mel, or sea-mew.
SCAN: to examine carefully.
SCANT: to cut short, to spare; scanty.
SCANTLING: a small portion, sample.
SCAPE: to escape. A slip, transgression.
SCATHE: injury, injure.
SCATHFUL: destructive, harmful.
SCONCE: the head, protection, a fort.
SCOTCH: to bruise or cut slightly.
SCRIMER: a fencer.
SCROYLE: a scabby fellow, scoundrel.
SCULL: a shoal of fish.
SEAL: set one's seal to a deed; confirm. A token.

SEAM: fat.

SEAMY: showing the seam, the worst side.

SEAR: scorched, withered. To dry up.

SEARCH: to probe (a wound).

SECT: a cutting or scion. A political party.

SEEL: to sew up the eyes, to blind.

SEEMING: outward manner and appearance.

SEEN: versed, instructed.

SELD: seldom.

SELF-BOUNTY: native goodness.

SEMBLABLY: alike.

SENIORY: seniority.

SENNET: a flourish of trumpets.

SEPULCHRE: to bury.

SEQUESTRATION: separation.

SERE: dry, withered.

SERJEANT: a bailiff.

SERPICO: a skin disease.

SERVICEABLE: diligent in service.

SETEBOS: a fiend feared by Caliban.

SETTER: a spy for thieves.

SEVERAL: privately owned land; enclosed pasture.

SHARDS: shreds, broken fragments of pottery.

SHARDS: the wing cases of beetles.

SHARKED: snatched up, collected hastily.

SHEER: pure. Unmixed.

SHENT: rebuked, blamed. Hurt.

SHERIFF'S-POST: a post at the door of a sheriff, to which royal proclamations were fixed.

SHIVE: slice.

SHOT: the reckoning at an ale-house.

SHOUGHS: shaggy dogs.

SHOVEL-BOARD: game played by sliding metal pieces along a board at a mark.

SHREWD: mischievous, shrewish.

SHRIFT: confession. Absolution.

SHRIVE: to hear or make confession.

SHROUD: protect, cover, hide.

SIEGE: seat. Stool. Rank.

SIGHT: an aperture in a helmet. A visor.

SIGHTLESS: invisible. Unsightly.

SILLY: simple, rustic.

SIMULAR: counterfeit, feigned. A simulator.

SINGLE: feeble.

SIR: a title often applied to a bachelor of arts and priests as well as to knights.

SITH: since.

SITHENCE: since.

SIZES: allowances.

SKAINS-MATES: scapegraces.

SKILL: to be of importance, to matter.

SKIMBLE-SKAMBLE: rambling, disjointed.

SKINKER: a drawer of liquor.

SKIRR: to scour.

SLAVE: to enslave.

SLEAVE: skein of silk.

SLEDDED: sledged.

SLEIDED: untwisted, raw, applied to silk.

SLIP: a counterfeit coin.

SLIPPER: slippery.

SLIVER: split, tear off. A branch.

SLOPS: loose breeches.

SLUBBER: to perform hurriedly. To smear.

SMOOTH: to flatter.

SNEAP: rebuke, snub, pinch.

SNECK-UP: go hang!

SNUFF: anger. 'Take in snuff', take offence.

SOFTLY: gently.

SOIL: spot, tarnish.

SOLICIT: solicitation.

SOLIDARE: a small coin.

SOMETIMES: formerly, former.

SOOTH: truth. Conciliation.

SOREL: a buck of the third year.

SORRY: sorrowful, dismal.

SORT: a company. Rank, condition. Lot. 'In a sort', in a manner.

SORT: to choose. to suit. To consort. To ordain.

SOT: fool, drunkard.

SOUL-FEARING: terrifying.

SOWL: to lug, drag.

SOWTER: name of a dog.

SPED: settled, done for.

SPEED: fortune.

SPERR: to bolt, fasten.

SPIAL: spy.

SPILL: to destroy.

SPILTH: spilling.

SPLEEN: violent feeling; anger, irritability, laughter.

SPRAG: quick.

SPRINGHALT: stringhalt, a disease of horses.

SPRITED: haunted.

SPURS: roots of trees.

SQUARE: to quarrel, measure.

SQUARE: the front part of a woman's dress.

SQUARE: fair, straightforward.

SQUARER: quarreller, swaggerer.

SQUASH: an unripe peascod.

SQUIER: a square or rule.

SQUINY: to squint.

STAGGERS: a disease in horses, attended with giddiness.

STAIN: to disfigure, tarnish.

STALE: a decoy. A gull. A prostitute.

STALE: urine.

STANIEL: an inferior kind of hawk.

STATE: a canopied chair.

STATION: attitude, stance.

STATIST: a statesman.

STATUTE-CAPS: woollen caps worn by citizens.

STEAD: to help, to act instead.

STEELED: set or fixed, delineated.

STERNAGE: steerage, course.

STICKLER: an arbitrator in combats.

STIGMATIC: branded by deformity.

STILL: constant.

STILLY: softly, silently.

STINT: to stop, to check.

STITHY: a smith's forge. To forge.

STOCCADO: a stoccata, or thrust in fencing.

STOCK: thrust.

STOMACH: courage. Appetite, inclination.

STONE-BOW: a cross-bow for throwing stones.

STOUP: a cup, flagon.

STOVER: fodder.

STRAIGHT: immediately.

STRAIN: lineage. Disposition. To embrace.

STRANGE: foreign. Coy, reserved. Marvellous.

STRANGENESS: coyness, reserve.

STRANGER: foreigner.

STRAPPADO: a kind of punishment.

STRICTURE: strictness.

STROSSERS: trousers.

STUCK: a sword-thrust (from stoccata).

STY: to lodge as in a sty.

SUBSCRIBE: to yield, succumb, write down.

SUCCESS: issue, consequence. Succession.

SUDDEN: hasty, rash.

SUFFERANCE: suffering, forbearance.

SUGGEST: to tempt, entice, persuade.

SUGGESTION: temptation, incitement.

SUITED: dressed.

SULLEN: doleful, melancholy.

SUMPTER: a pack-horse, drudge.

SUPPOSE: supposition, substitution.

SUPPOSED: counterfeit.

SURCEASE: cessation, death.

SURPRISE: to capture by surprise.

SUR-REINED: over-worked.

SUSPECT: suspicion.

SUSPIRE: to breathe.

SWABBER: a sweeper of the deck of a ship.

SWARTH: black.

SWARTH: quantity of grass cut down by one
  sweep of the scythe.

SWASHER: swaggerer.

SWATH: The same as 'swarth'.

SWATHLING: swaddling.

SWAY: to move on, advance.

SWIFT: ready, quick.

SWINGE-BUCKLER: a bully, a swashbuckler.

TABLE: a tablet, note-book, painting surface.

TABLES: the game of backgammon. A note-book.

TABOR: a small side-drum.

TABOURINE: tambourine, drum.

TAG: the rabble.

TAINT: stain, defile; be infected by.

TAINTURE: defilement.

TAKE: to infect, bewitch.

TAKE OUT: to copy.

TAKE UP: to borrow money, or buy on credit. To make up a quarrel.

TAKING: infection, malignant influence.

TAKING OFF: murder.

TALE: counting, reckoning.

TALL: strong, valiant.

TALLOW-CATCH: a lump of tallow.

TANG: twang, sound.

TANLING: anything tanned by the sun.

TARRE: to excite, urge on.

TARRIANCE: delay.

TARTAR: Tartarus, hell.

TASK: to employ. Challenge.

TASKING: challenging.

TASTE: enjoy sexually.

TAWDRY-LACE: a rustic necklace.

TAXATION: satire, sarcasm. Demand.

TAXING: satire, censure.

TEEN: grief.

TELL: to count.

TEMPER: to mix, to soften.

TEMPERANCE: temperature.

TEND: to attend to.

TENDER: offer, desire, esteem. To have consideration for.

TENT: to probe as a wound.

TERCEL: the male of the goshawk.

TERMAGANT: a ranting character in old plays.

TESTED: pure, assayed.

TESTERN: to reward with a tester, or six-pence.

THARBOROUGH: (corrupted from 'third-borough') a constable.

THEORICK: theory.

THEWS: sinews, muscles.

THICK: (of speech) huskily.

THICK-PLEACHED: thickly intertwined.

THIRD-BOROUGH: a constable.

THOUGHT: anxiety, grief.

THRASONICAL: boastful.

THREE-MAN BEETLE: a wooden mallet worked by three men.

THREE-MAN-SONG-MEN: singers of glees in three parts.

THREE-PILE: three-piled velvet.

THRENE: lament.

THRID: thread, fibre.

THROE: to put in agonies, cause pain.

THRUM: the tufted end of a thread in weaving.

THRUMMED: made of coarse ends or tufts.

TICKLE: ticklish.

TIGHT: nimble, active. Water-tight.

TIKE: a cur.

TILLY-VALLY: an exclamation of contempt.

TILTH: tillage.

TIMELESS: untimely.

TINCT: stain, dye.Colour of the elixir of life.

TIRE: attire, head-dress.

TIRE: to tear as a bird of prey. Devour.

TIRE: attire, headdress.

TOD: a tod of wool (28lbs).

TOKENED: marked with plague spots.

TOKENS: plague spots; marks of infection.

TOLL: to exact toll. To pay toll.

TOPLESS: supreme, without superior.

TOUCH: touchstone. Trait. An acute feeling.

TOUCHED: pricked, infected.

TOUSE: to pull, tear.

TOWARD: nearly ready, impending.

TOYS: trifles, foolish tricks.

TRADE: beaten path.

TRAJECT: a ferry.

TRANSLATED: transformed.

TRASH: to check, as a huntsman his hounds.

TRAY-TRIP: an old game played with dice.

TREACHERS: traitors, deceivers.

TREATIES: entreaties.

TRENCHED: carved, engraved.

TRICK: fashion. Distinguishing characteristic. Knack.

TRICK: to dress up.

TRICKED: blazoned, spotted.

TRICKING: ornament, costumes.

TRICKSY: elegantly.

TRIPLE: third.

TROJAN: a cant word for a thief.

TROLL-MY-DAMES: (Fr. *trou-madame*;) a game like bagatelle.

TROTH-PLIGHT: betrothed.

TROW: to trust, think.

TRUE: honest.

TRUNDLE-TAIL: a long-tailed dog.

TUCKET-SONANCE: a flourish on the trumpet.

TUNDISH: a funnel.

TURLYGOOD: bedlam-beggars, gypsies.

TWIGGEN: made of twigs, wicker.

TWILLED: Retained by woven branches.

TWINK: a twinkling.

TWIRE: to peep.

UMBERED: stained, dark, as with umber.

UNANELED: without extreme unction.

UNAVOIDED: unavoidable.

UNBARBED: uncovered, bare.

UNBATED: unblunted.

UNBOLT: to disclose, explain.

UNBOLTED: unsifted, unrefined.

UNBREATHED: unpractised.

UNCAPE: to throw off the hounds.

UNCHARGED: undefended, acquitted.

UNCLEW: to unravel, undo.

UNCOINED: unalloyed, unfeigned.

UNDERGO: to undertake.

UNDERTAKER: one who takes up another's quarrel.

UNDER-WROUGHT: undermined.

UNEATH: hardly.

UNEXPRESSIVE: inexpressible, beyond praise.

UNFAIR: to deprive of beauty.

UNHATCHED: undisclosed.

UNHOUSELED: without receiving the sacrament.

UNIMPROVED: undisciplined, inexperienced.

UNION: a pearl.

UNKIND: unnatural.

UNLIVED: bereft of life.

UNMANNED: untamed, applied to a hawk.

UNOWED: unowned.

UNPREGNANT: unready to act.

UNPROPER: common to all, not one's own.

UNQUESTIONABLE: averse to questioning.

UNREADY: undressed.

UNRESPECTIVE: inconsiderate. Undiscriminating.

UNSISTING: unresisting.

UNSTANCHED: incontinent.

UNTEMPERING: unsoftening.

UNTENTED: unsearchable, incurable.

UNTRADED: unused, uncommon.

UNVALUED: priceless. Of little value.

UPSPRING REEL: a boisterous dance.

URCHIN: the hedge-hog.

USANCE: usury.

USE: interest, custom, trust.

UTIS: merriment which accompanied a festival.

UTTER: to expel, put forth, sell.

UTTERANCE: extremity, the bitter end.

VADE: to fade.

VAIL: to lower, submit. Sinking.

VALANCED: fringed (with a beard).

VALIDITY: value, worth.

VANTAGE: advantage.

VANTBRACE: armour for the forearm.

VARLET: a servant, valet. A rascal.

VAST: waste, desert.

VASTIDITY: immensity.

VASTY: vast, immense.

VAUNT: the van, the beginning.

VAUNT-COURIERS: forerunners.

VAWARD: the van, vanguard, advanced guard.

VEGETIVES: herbs, vegetables.

VELURE: velvet.

VELVET-GUARDS: velvet trimmings; applied metaphorically to the citizens who wore them.

VENEW: a bout in fencing, a term applied to repartee and sallies of wit.

VENGE: to avenge.

VENTAGES: holes in a flute or flageolet.

VERY: true, real.

VIA: away!

VICE: the buffoon in the old morality plays.

VIE: to challenge a term at cards. To compete.

VIEWLESS: invisible.

VILLAIN: a lowborn man: a scoundrel.

VINEWED: mouldy.

VIOL-DE-GAMBOYS: a bass viol.

VIRGINALLING: playing with the fingers, as on the virginals.

VIRTUE: the essential excellence. Valour.

VIRTUOUS: excellent, potent.

219

VIZAMENT: advisement, counsel.
VOLUBLE: fickle.
VOTARIST: votary, one who has taken a vow.
VULGAR: the common people.
VULGARLY: publicly.

WAFT: to wave, beckon. To turn, carry by sea.
WAFTAGE: passage by water.
WAFTURE: waving, beckoning.
WAGE: to reward as with wages.
WAILFUL: lamentable.
WAIST: the middle of a ship.
WANNION: 'With a wannion' — 'with a vengeance'.
WAPPENED: withered, overworn.
WARD: guard. Prison. Safety.
WARDEN: a large pear used for baking.
WARDER: truncheon, staff.
WARN: to summon.
WASSAIL: a drinking bout. Festivity.
WAT: a familiar word for a hare.
WATCH: a watch light. Wakefulness.
WATCH: to tame by keeping constantly awake.
WATER-GALL: a secondary rainbow.
WATER-RUG: a kind of dog.
WATER-WORK: painting in distemper or water colour.
WAX: to grow.
WEATHER-FEND: defend from the weather, shelter.
WEB AND PIN: the cataract in the eye.
WEE: to think.
WEED: garment.

WEET: to know.

WELKIN: the sky; sky-blue.

WELL-LIKING: in good condition, plump.

WEND: to go.

WESAND: the wind-pipe.

WHELK: a weal, pimple.

WHELKED: marked with whelks or protuberances.

WHEN: an exclamation of impatience.

WHIFFLER: an officer who clears the way in processions.

WHILE-ERE: a little while ago.

WHILES: until.

WHIP-STOCK: handle of a whip.

WHIST: hushed, silent.

WHITE: the centre of an archery butt.

WHITELY: pale-faced.

WHITING-TIME: bleaching time.

WHITSTER: bleacher.

WHITTLE: a clasp knife.

WHOO-BUB: hubbub.

WIDOW: to endow with a widow's right.

WIDOWHOOD: widow's jointure.

WIGHT: person.

WILDERNESS: wildness.

WIMPLED: veiled, hooded, blindfolded.

WINDOW-BARS: lattice-work across a woman's stomacher.

WINDRING: winding.

WINTER-GROUND: to protect (a plant) from frost.

WIS: in the compound 'I wis', certainly.

WISTLY: wistfully.

WIT: knowledge, wisdom.

WITHOUT: beyond.

WITS: five, the five senses.

WITTOL: a contented cuckold.

WITTY: intelligent.

WOMAN-TIRED: hen-pecked.

WONDERED: marvellously gifted.

WOOD: mad.

WOODCOCK: a simpleton.

WOODMAN: a hunter; so, of women.

WOOLWARD: shirtless.

WORD: flatter or put off with words. The Bible.

WORLD: 'To go to the world', to get married; 'a woman of the world', a married woman.

WORM: a serpent.

WORTS: cabbages.

WOT: to know.

WOUND: twisted about.

WREAK: vengeance. To avenge.

WREAKFUL: revengeful, avenging.

WREST: an instrument for tuning a harp. To devise, pervert.

WRIT: gospel, truth. Document.

WRITHLED: shrivelled, wrinkled.

WROTH: misfortune.

WRUNG: twisted, strained.

WRY: to swerve, to go astray.

YARE: ready, swift, easily handled.

YARELY: readily, nimbly.

Y-CLAD: clad.

Y-CLEPED: called, named.

YEARN: to grieve, vex.

YELLOWNESS: jealousy.

YELLOWS: a disease of horses.

YEOMAN: a sheriff's officer. A freeholder or farmer.

YIELD: to reward. To report.

YOND: yonder.

ZANY: a clown, gull. A fool's stooge.

Notes

Notes

Notes

Notes